Happy reading and crafting!

Kelly A. [illegible]

SPAM

Edible

Series Editor: Andrew F. Smith

EDIBLE is a revolutionary series of books dedicated to food and drink that explores the rich history of cuisine. Each book reveals the global history and culture of one type of food or beverage.

Already published

Apple Erika Janik, *Avocado* Jeff Miller, *Banana* Lorna Piatti-Farnell, *Barbecue* Jonathan Deutsch and Megan J. Elias, *Beans* Nathalie Rachel Morris, *Beef* Lorna Piatti-Farnell, *Beer* Gavin D. Smith, *Berries* Heather Arndt Anderson, *Biscuits and Cookies* Anastasia Edwards, *Brandy* Becky Sue Epstein, *Bread* William Rubel, *Breakfast Cereal* Kathryn Cornell Dolan, *Cabbage* Meg Muckenhoupt, *Cake* Nicola Humble, *Cannabis* Bradley J. Borougerdi, *Caviar* Nichola Fletcher, *Champagne* Becky Sue Epstein, *Cheese* Andrew Dalby, *Chillies* Heather Arndt Anderson, *Chocolate* Sarah Moss and Alexander Badenoch, *Cocktails* Joseph M. Carlin, *Coconut* Constance L. Kirker and Mary Newman, *Cod* Elisabeth Townsend, *Coffee* Jonathan Morris, *Corn* Michael Owen Jones, *Curry* Colleen Taylor Sen, *Dates* Nawal Nasrallah, *Doughnut* Heather Delancey Hunwick, *Dumplings* Barbara Gallani, *Edible Flowers* Constance L. Kirker and Mary Newman, *Edible Insects* Gina Louise Hunter, *Eggs* Diane Toops, *Fats* Michelle Phillipov, *Figs* David C. Sutton, *Foie Gras* Norman Kolpas, *Game* Paula Young Lee, *Gin* Lesley Jacobs Solmonson, *Hamburger* Andrew F. Smith, *Herbs* Gary Allen, *Herring* Kathy Hunt, *Honey* Lucy M. Long, *Hot Dog* Bruce Kraig, *Hummus* Harriet Nussbaum, *Ice Cream* Laura B. Weiss, *Jam, Jelly and Marmalade* Sarah B. Hood, *Lamb* Brian Yarvin, *Lemon* Toby Sonneman, *Liqueur* Lesley Jacobs Solmonson, *Lobster* Elisabeth Townsend, *Mango* Constance L. Kirker and Mary Newman, *Melon* Sylvia Lovegren, *Milk* Hannah Velten, *Moonshine* Kevin R. Kosar, *Mushroom* Cynthia D. Bertelsen, *Mustard* Demet Güzey, *Nuts* Ken Albala, *Offal* Nina Edwards, *Olive* Fabrizia Lanza, *Onions and Garlic* Martha Jay, *Oranges* Clarissa Hyman, *Oyster* Carolyn Tillie, *Pancake* Ken Albala, *Pasta and Noodles* Kantha Shelke, *Pickles* Jan Davison, *Pie* Janet Clarkson, *Pineapple* Kaori O'Connor, *Pizza* Carol Helstosky, *Pomegranate* Damien Stone, *Pork* Katharine M. Rogers, *Potato* Andrew F. Smith, *Pudding* Jeri Quinzio, *Rice* Renee Marton, *Rum* Richard Foss, *Saffron* Ramin Ganeshram, *Salad* Judith Weinraub, *Salmon* Nicolaas Mink, *Sandwich* Bee Wilson, *Sauces* Maryann Tebben, *Sausage* Gary Allen, *Seaweed* Kaori O'Connor, *Shrimp* Yvette Florio Lane, *Soda and Fizzy Drinks* Judith Levin, *Soup* Janet Clarkson, *Spices* Fred Czarra, *SPAM* Kelly A. Spring, *Sweets and Candy* Laura Mason, *Tea* Helen Saberi, *Tequila* Ian Williams, *Tomato* Clarissa Hyman, *Truffle* Zachary Nowak, *Vanilla* Rosa Abreu-Runkel, *Vodka* Patricia Herlihy, *Water* Ian Miller, *Whiskey* Kevin R. Kosar, *Wine* Marc Millon, *Yoghurt* June Hersh

SPAM

A Global History

Kelly A. Spring

REAKTION BOOKS

In loving memory, to my grandmother, June D. Codding (1932–2023), who understood the importance of food, and history, to Dr Paul H. Plotz (1937–2024), who invented SPAM strudel, and to Dr Marci Freedman (1985–2024), who kept Kosher, but understood the value of SPAM

Published by Reaktion Books Ltd
Unit 32, Waterside
44–48 Wharf Road
London N1 7UX, UK
www.reaktionbooks.co.uk

First published 2025

EU GPSR Authorised Representative
LOGOS EUROPE, 9 rue Nicolas Poussin, 17000, La Rochelle, France
email: contact@logoseurope.eu

Printed and bound in India by Replika Press Pvt. Ltd

A catalogue record for this book is available from the British Library

ISBN 978 1 83639 066 4

Contents

A can of Hormel's original SPAM®.

Foreword

SPAM® has existed quietly in the background of my life for many years, popping up occasionally in unexpected ways. I first encountered SPAM in my teens in the United States, when I was on a camping trip with my family. The tinned meat was introduced as a new food that could be easily carried and used while camping because it didn't require refrigeration. It was also conveniently rendered eatable by frying it over an open fire, making it an inexpensive meal that required little preparation and cooking. The taste, however, was another matter. Though not nearly as bad as liver and onions, another parental experiment in eating, the warmed-up congealed meat did not appeal to my sister or me. Having had it once, we decided that we had had enough for a lifetime. Never again, we vowed, would we deign to buy, let alone eat, the processed pork.

Fast forward a decade to South Korea, where I found myself teaching English as a foreign language in a few universities in Seoul. One would little expect to find SPAM on the other side of the globe. But there it was, sitting on the shelf of many supermarkets throughout the country. Even more to my astonishment, special gift sets of SPAM were available in shops and bought as presents during traditional Korean holidays. The manifestation of these sets and the presence of SPAM in grocery stores is part of the long legacy of the Korean War, and the triumph over adversity. Hostilities may have halted, but the Koreans' wartime food inheritance from the American military lives on in South Korea.

Five years later, SPAM reared up again in the UK as I was studying British foodways of the Second World War for my PhD in modern history. Less widespread than in Korea, SPAM nevertheless made itself known in little ways. I would find it occasionally among the Second World War diarists that I read, the oral history interviews that I conducted and the wartime propaganda that I researched.[1] Here, too, SPAM stood on present-day supermarket shelves, echoing its wartime past, while making itself available to future generations. It symbolized the food insecurity of the war, and the continuing impact of American culture on British cuisine.

Seeing SPAM not through the lens of a cheap food in a modern, food-secure society but through the historical context of a vitally important source of calories in wartime, I began to shift my perspective of the tinned meat. Understanding the food in terms of the historically important role it has played enabled me to gain a grudging respect for its place in global food history. The wide spectrum of views that people held about SPAM around the world intrigued me, generating a kernel of interest for possible future exploration, when time permitted, in my researcher's brain. This book is the outcome of that kernel. This is a book that charts SPAM's history from its domestic beginnings to its status as an enduring symbol of war and the spread of American foodways around the world.

I enjoyed the experience of exploring the depths of this unassuming food, which had a tremendous impact on the world and remains a product consumed in multiple countries today. I hope you will find its history and the enduring pop culture associated with it as interesting and diverting as I have.

Introduction

SPAM is a law unto itself. It is hard to define, and for many, even harder to fathom consuming. But it is one of the most recognizable and iconic American foods, along with other famous brands, including the soft drink Coca-Cola and Hershey's chocolate bars. Born in 1937 and produced in Austin, Minnesota, SPAM is very much a product of its upbringing in the latter phase of the Great Depression, when resources, financial and material, were stretched thinly in many households. Food-manufacturing companies, such as Hormel®, looked for ways to capture the consumer market, while utilizing the means available to it in the economic downturn to make a profit. In these social and economic contexts, the industrialization of food was a growing and highly effective way to provide consumables that would last longer and cost less for families in reduced circumstances. SPAM burst onto the scene in this climate, adding to the company's evolving offerings for the consumer market.

SPAM comes in an oblong 340-gram (12 oz) tin and looks very much like what it is – a pink slab of processed, pressed and pre-cooked pork. Detractors of the tinned product have often likened it to a form of 'mystery meat' reminiscent of meat products described in Upton Sinclair's *The Jungle* (1906), a fictionalized account of the horrific working conditions in the meat-packing industry in Chicago, Illinois, at the turn of the twentieth century.[1] But the Hormel Corporation has always striven to meet or exceed federal health regulations surrounding the production of the product. Contrary to urban myth, the food is not made up of unknown, or unwanted, parts of a pig. Rather, SPAM consists of only a handful of ingredients, unlike many other foods available on the market today, which are full of chemicals and nearly unpronounceable materials. Classic SPAM consists of just six ingredients: namely, pork with ham, salt, water, modified potato starch, sugar and sodium nitrite. This recipe has remained virtually unchanged for more than eighty years, except with the addition of modified potato starch, which eliminates the layer of fat found in the original tins of SPAM.

The process to produce SPAM is relatively straightforward and highly automated. First, the ingredients are mixed, and then dispersed into oblong tins. The tins are then sealed, cooked in a water bath cooled over a three-hour period. Finally, they are labelled, packaged and shipped to distributors around the world.[2]

Approximately 12.8 tins of SPAM are eaten every second of the day around the globe.[3] SPAM is sold all over the United States and in U.S. territories, including Puerto Rico, Guam and American Samoa, as well as the Pacific islands of the Solomon Islands and Saipan. In total, SPAM is available in 48 countries across the world, including Canada, Mexico, Colombia, the United Kingdom, South Korea, the Philippines, Hong Kong, China, Japan, Malaysia, Indonesia, Australia and New Zealand.

Minnesota is not the only domestic location in which SPAM is now produced. It is also manufactured in Dubuque, Iowa. In order to satisfy the large demand abroad, SPAM is also produced and distributed by manufacturers that have a licence from Hormel International to do so in other countries, including China (Hormel (China) Investment Co., Ltd), South Korea (CJ CheilJedang Corp) and the Philippines (San Miguel Corp. (SMC)), which is Hormel's largest international joint venture. In addition to Classic SPAM, the tinned meat currently comes in eleven other varieties, which include SPAM with real Hormel Bacon, SPAM Oven Roasted Turkey, SPAM Hickory Smoke Flavored, SPAM Teriyaki, SPAM Hot & Spicy and SPAM Chorizo. Due to the overwhelming popularity of SPAM in Korea and Korean cooking, Hormel added SPAM Korean BBQ Flavored in 2024. In addition to the twelve types of SPAM available on the market today, Hormel has also created a variety of limited-edition versions of SPAM to mark holidays, the company's anniversaries and other special events associated with the brand (more details on these varieties are available in Chapter Six).

SPAM wall, Toronto, 2006.

Over the course of its history, more than 9 billion tins of Hormel's SPAM have been sold and eaten by the world's population. The Second World War propelled SPAM beyond the national stage and onto the world market, helping the Hormel Corporation not only to survive but to thrive during the conflict. SPAM's central role in feeding the U.S. home front and military front as well as the Allies has had a long-term impact on the company, as well as on people and cultures around the world in the twentieth and twenty-first centuries. It has also acted and continues to act as a form of U.S. gastrodiplomacy, wielding America's soft power and influence in many corners of the world where SPAM is still bought and consumed. Beyond just a form of protein and sustaining nourishment – albeit one that is potentially detrimental to health if eaten in large quantities – SPAM also acts as a symbol of the Americanization of the globe. It projects a way of life through the United States' foodways, embodying an image of industrialization, uniformity, abundance and convenience in its wake.

This book aims to examine the varied and complex international history of SPAM from its 1937 beginnings to its global spike in sales during the 2020–23 pandemic. It explores the important links between war, food insecurity and American food relief. Specifically, the book uses SPAM as a lens to chart America's long-term influence on the people with whom and places in which it waged war. Through its food aid, specifically SPAM, the United States used soft diplomacy to spread its culture and values around the world. Direct assistance from the U.S. government as well as provisions carried by U.S. soldiers and given to local populations during the conflicts of the twentieth century had an impact on people's consumption practices and lifestyles, and subsequently their perceptions of America and American people. Through an investigation of this food, the book also explores the longevity of war on countries that were allied to, and in many cases, liberated and occupied by the U.S. military. Although hostilities ceased in these twentieth-century wars, SPAM continues to be eaten and enjoyed today in these former sites of conflict throughout the world.

The scope of this work is largely historical in nature. It provides the background and origins of SPAM as a local and national good produced by Hormel Foods in the years before the Second World War. It also looks at the pervasive reach of SPAM during the Second World War. The book traces how SPAM became a major component of food relief from the United States to its wartime Allies, and focuses on two theatres of military operations in the Second World War – Europe and the Pacific – to investigate how people living in these parts of the world obtained, used and responded to SPAM and, more broadly, to the Americans who provided this relief. The United Kingdom was the largest beneficiary of the U.S. aid programme Lend-Lease, and as such special attention will be paid to how the British perceived and employed SPAM on the home front. The Korean War became the next major war involving American soldiers, and here again the U.S. military provided the Korean populace with SPAM during the conflict.

The following chapters examine the popular memory of SPAM in a global context, illustrating the many festivals that are dedicated to preserving and perpetuating its consumption. Not only its enduring popularity, but its resurgence is explored: during the COVID-19 crisis of 2020–23, SPAM was once again on the menu in many countries as a long-lasting protein source. Finally, this book examines the dominant presence of Hormel in Austin, Minnesota, the birthplace of SPAM, and concludes with some SPAM recipes that showcase the diversity of the food across time and space.

View of the Commercial Slip end of the Central Wharf, Buffalo, New York, 1878.

I

SPAM to the Rescue: The Business and Politics of Processed Food

The history of the Hormel Corporation, and its most famous product, SPAM, is very much an American story of immigrants, who, over a few short generations, were able to achieve the ultimate American dream. In the 1800s, the United States experienced a massive influx of immigrants from Europe, swelling its population and adding to the mix of nationalities, languages and cultures that converged in the cities and towns across the country.

Immigrants tended to form communities with other immigrants from their home country when they settled in the United States. These ethnic groups brought their knowledge and skills to bear on their new surroundings, contributing much to the economic, political, social and cultural landscape of the communities in which they lived. Their efforts also helped to shape the foodways of their surroundings, often melding their cookery knowledge and culinary ingenuity from the Old World with the food offerings and consumption habits of the New World.

Throughout the nineteenth century, there was a massive influx of German immigrants into the USA, with 5 million making the transatlantic voyage by 1900.[1] Large groups of immigrant German families settled in the Northeast and Midwest, establishing their own homesteads.[2] Buffalo, a burgeoning city at the edge of western New York State, acted as a gateway to the Midwest, easily accessible by either land or water, via Lake Erie and the Erie Canal. Here too, a thriving German immigrant community took shape and grew from the early 1800s onwards.[3] The Germans living in the city contributed to its diverse industries, including tanning, milling and meat packing.

The Hormel family, like many other German families, was part of the German exodus to the United States during this period. The parents and grandparents of George A. Hormel, founder of what would become the Hormel Corporation, were among those who came to make a new life in America, his father's side emigrating in 1833 and his mother's in 1850, and they both settled in Buffalo. According to the company's official history, George A. Hormel's parents both hailed from northeast Germany. His father, John Hormel, was born in 1830 and raised in Schwalbach, near Frankfurt. His mother, Susanna Decker, was born in 1836 and raised in the town of Neuwied, near Schwalbach. The Decker and the Hormel families engaged in the interconnected trades most prevalent in Buffalo at that time; namely, the meat-packing and tanning industries. John and Susanna would later meet in Buffalo, marry and have George Hormel, who was born in 1860.[4]

The company's biography to celebrate its centenary relates how, as a young man, George Hormel travelled to Chicago, then the centre of the meat-packing industry in the United States, to work for his uncle Jay Decker in the meat-packing and distribution business. He later became a buyer of wool and hides for Oberne, Hosick & Company. His sales territory encompassed Iowa and southern Minnesota, which included Austin.[5] It was in Austin that Hormel was able to bring together all that he had learned from his experience in tanning and meat-packing to create a billion-dollar industry.

In Austin, Hormel began a co-owned meat-packing and sales venture in 1887, but the business failed five years later. Undeterred, George set up his own business, Geo. A. Hormel & Co., in 1891. From this unlikely beginning, Hormel built a company that focused primarily on the production and sale of pork products. After a decade in business, company records in 1901 show its net worth stood at over $93,200, which in today's currency is more than $3 million.[6]

The success of the company enabled Hormel to expand beyond state and national borders, adding to the business's profit margins and boosting its brand recognition. In the first decade of the twentieth century, the company opened seven distribution centres, including in San Antonio, Texas, and Atlanta, Georgia, as well as two more in Minnesota (Duluth and St Paul).[7] After a trip to the United Kingdom in 1905, George A. Hormel also set up an export business with Arthur E. Jones of Marples, Jones & Co, based in Liverpool, England.[8] These moves to expand the international reach of the company proved advantageous in the short term, as official company

Geo. A. Hormel & Co. plant, Austin, Minnesota, 1910.

figures show that as much as a third of all company sales came from exports to Britain during and after the First World War.[9] Such sales of Hormel products in the war served to augment meat levels in the UK, which were curtailed and later rationed due to wartime necessities as well as intensified German submarine activities over the course of the conflict. The long-term implications of Hormel brand recognition, sales and consumption of Hormel foods in the UK would become crucial a couple of decades later. As we will see in the third chapter, the importance of these early export measures laid the foundation for the food links that would help to sustain Britain in the Second World War.

This period in the evolution and expansion of U.S. business was punctuated by improved mechanization and increased speed of production, which was characterized by Henry Ford's industrial innovation of the assembly line and standardized manufacturing techniques. Utilizing these new methods reduced waste of materials, kept labour costs down and produced goods that were more affordable to the average consumer. The Hormel Corporation, no doubt wishing to take advantage of such a revolution in the industry, sought to refine its processes and create new products, which could be inexpensively produced and have a long shelf life so as to support the needs of its customers. Jay Hormel, son of George A. Hormel, was born in 1892 and joined the family business in the second decade of the new century, when he was in his twenties. He sought to develop tinned products as an extension of the company's meat-processing activities. According to the company's history, in 1926, with the help of a German expert in tinned meat, Paul Joern, Hormel was able to produce the first tinned ham for sale in the United States.[10] Hormel's innovations made its tinned foods long lasting and easily transportable across great distances, enabling it to expand its business in new directions, have a much more significant reach and raise the status and brand recognition of its products nationally and internationally. The expansion of its food line to include these inexpensive and filling products would prove invaluable to both the company and the people who consumed the foods in the coming economic catastrophe of the Great Depression.

From the latter part of 1929 until almost the start of the Second World War, the people of the United States – and indeed, of the entire world – were facing the severe effects of the Great Depression. Many suffered huge losses, financial and personal, when the stock market crashed, banks closed and businesses folded. Over the next decade, millions of people lost their jobs and life savings. At the height of the economic downturn in 1933, one-quarter of all workers in the United States were unemployed, which equated to nearly 13 million people.[11] Many Americans were thrown into poverty and food insecurity. And those who were still able to find work did not go unscathed, as wages fell more than 40 per cent.[12]

A system of social welfare did not exist at this time, and many people found themselves on the breadline; charities such as the Salvation Army and volunteer organizations opened a record number of soup kitchens, which proliferated across the United States to feed those who could no longer afford to feed themselves.

Due to their limited financial resources, many families looked to buy inexpensive, mass-produced foods, which would enable them to stretch their dollars while filling their stomachs. Hormel proved remarkably adept at adapting to this need in the market, adding the tinned goods that quickly became popular and in demand. Over the next decade, the company created additional products, which are well known today, to augment its tinned offerings. Important brands that were produced include Dinty Moore® Beef Stew and Chili Con Carne,

Men in line at a soup kitchen during the Great Depression, June 1936.

both created by Hormel in 1935. Arguably, the greatest and best-known Hormel food that came to fruition in the Great Depression was SPAM. SPAM surpassed its tinned cousins in notoriety and sales volume, and provided a vital source of protein for consumers in constrained economic circumstances. The Hormel corporation created a 340-gram (12 oz) tin of processed pork to take advantage of the large amount of pork shoulder meat that the company accumulated in the process of producing other foodstuffs and that was underutilized and often discarded. In search of a new brand name for the product, Hormel held a competition with a $100 cash prize for the person who could come up with a catchy name for the new product. The winner of the prize, Kenneth Daigneau, the brother of the vice president of the company, R. H. Daigneau, came up with the moniker 'SPAM'.[13]

There has been much conjecture as to the meaning of the word. Some suggest that 'SPAM' is a portmanteau of 'spiced ham', and indeed Hormel had sought to bring forth something akin to a tinned spiced ham in creating this product. Other interpretations of the name include 'Spiced Pork and Ham' and even 'Specially Processed American Meat'. However, Hormel has never revealed the actual meaning or origin of the name.

Regardless of the story behind the name, the actual food, which was first produced in the summer of 1937, was a huge success, bringing a large amount of revenue to the company.[14] Much of this success rested on the large and effective marketing effort that the Hormel Corporation put into promoting the product, advertising it in a wide variety of national newspapers and magazines and on the radio; these advertisements were often targeted at wives and mothers, as they held the primary responsibility for feeding their families.[15] Hormel's concerted activities to appeal to women through its SPAM marketing campaigns are evident in a *Good Housekeeping* advertisement of 1939, in which customers are instructed to 'Keep Cool – Just Open a Can of SPAM'. Placed next to a romance story, and preceded and followed by other adverts for items geared towards women, such as baby food, detergent and beauty products, the advert advised women on quick ways to cater for unexpected dinner guests. The company endeavoured to build long-term brand recognition and product use by projecting the message that their tinned food would support women in their domestic duties by saving them time and energy around meal preparation. The *Good Housekeeping* advert also allowed Hormel to alert female readers to their new SPAM cookbook. Offering the cookbook for free served as an additional means by which the company could encourage women to buy SPAM, ensuring long-term brand loyalty. The cookbook was not only a marketing gimmick, but a useful guide on how to prepare this novel food in creative ways.

Hormel also took advantage of one of the most popular forms of entertainment at the time: radio. They sponsored

"I don't know what I am," said Margaret a little pettishly.

"I must look a sight," said Susan. "Where's my handbag? I had it when we came in. There it is, on the mantel. Get it for me, Maggie, dear."

Margaret took the few steps to the mantel. She thought the tessellated floor moved under her feet. She thought, as she looked down, that water crept up along the lines of the patterned oak. How could it? Was there a new sound in the house, a gurgle of water under the floor, a steady slap-slap?

"You know, Eddie reminds me a lot of Robert," Susan was saying as Margaret handed her the bag. She poked a finger under the rhinestone clasp and spread the bag open. "I hadn't thought of it before. What happened to Robert, Maggie?"

"He died. He got typhoid in that mining camp." ("Where he went because of you: tell her!") Margaret stood close to the couch.

"Dead?" Susan looked up, a vanity case open in one hand. "I didn't know." There was a crease between her plucked, accented brows. "He would be an old man now, wouldn't he? He was older than you—or me. I never thought of that before." She shrugged. "I don't like elderly men.

"Robert—ah, he didn't have to grow old! He was beautiful. Eddie isn't really like him. Why, I remember the row they made about Robert, right here in this room! Father and Mother—about Susan Lathrop and her *groom!* I didn't care, I loved him. But he cared, he was furious. He went away, West. I would have waited forever—at least I thought so." She began to spat powder over her face, the scent strong for a moment. "But I couldn't stand his taking the money."

"What money?" Margaret leaned closer.

Susan's voice had dropped. It was an unhappy whisper against the background of steady noise around them. Susan set her lips together and dusted her chin.

"What money?" urged Margaret.

"The money my father gave him, if he'd go off. I—I suppose he was poor—"

"Is that what they told you?" Margaret's scorn brought Susan's eyes up from the mirror. "You might have known it was a lie! Robert never took a cent except his wages. Why, I sent him money that year, when I began to teach—money for food!"

"I might have known," said Susan slowly. "I wasn't so smart then. Why, Maggie, it's like a present! Everything was criss-cross, and we're laying it all straight."

"WHEN he died, his landlady sent me his things," said Margaret. "His account book, and a picture of you—and a letter. I would never give you the letter."

"I don't want to see the picture!" Susan peered again into the little mirror; she fished a lipstick out of the bag. She made a stroke with the pencil, but her hand wavered, and the crimson was a clown's mouth. Angrily she dabbed at it with a handkerchief, sticking out the point of her tongue to moisten a corner. "I don't care how I look," she said. She dropped the lipstick, mirror, handkerchief, into the purse, and pinched the rhinestones shut. "I've been a fool, haven't I? But you have to have somebody to love as long as you live, don't you?" Her voice was warm again, and clear. "Whatever they've been, I've had the loving of them. Nobody can take that away!"

Margaret had drawn away from the divan, her shoulders hunched, her hands doubled into fists. She wanted to listen to Susan, but something, *something* was moving past the windows at the end of the room, was looking in. She walked toward the windows, slowly, not to frighten Susan, her feet slipping in the water.

'Keep Cool – Just Open a Can of SPAM', *Good Housekeeping*, CIX/1 (July 1939).

George Burns and his wife, Gracie Allen, *c.* 1952.

adverts and radio programmes, including *It Happened in Hollywood*, which debuted on the broadcasting service CBS in 1937, and the very popular *The Burns and Allen Show* on NBC, starring the married comedic couple Gracie Allen and George Burns. Embedded in the programmes' jokes and skits was the promotion of SPAM.[16] The far-reaching marketing campaigns led to a great uptake of Hormel's product by the American public, and the consumption of SPAM in U.S. households from 1937 to 1940 jumped by 52 per cent.[17]

The Great Depression and the hardships faced by the American public laid the foundation for Hormel's innovative approach to food waste and its savvy response to consumer demand. As a result, SPAM became a ubiquitous part of U.S. foodways of the late 1930s and early 1940s. It would be the tinned food's well-placed position in the food market as well as its convenient packaging and long shelf life that would enable it to become one of the most recognized American products of the twentieth century.

2
SPAM and the March to War

Germany's invasion of Poland in September 1939 marked the start of the Second World War. During the conflict, as hostilities escalated to spread across the globe, Britain, France and the other Allied countries mobilized their forces against the militaries of the Axis powers – Germany, Italy and Japan. Military and home front boundaries blurred as the public was drawn into the war effort in a variety of ways, from civilians serving as munitions workers to those undertaking active combat duty. By the spring of 1940, German soldiers had rumbled over much of Europe, conquering France and the Low Countries, and pushing British troops back across the Channel. In July of that same year, the Battle of Britain got under way, with the bombardment of the British home front by the German Blitzkrieg, while German U-boat action created heavy losses at sea for the British Navy and Merchant Navy. Britain, which was not agriculturally self-sufficient, faced food insecurity as a result of the attacks at sea.

In 1940 the newly appointed prime minister Winston Churchill turned to the USA for help, pleading for financial and material aid to sustain the UK's military and domestic exertions in the face of the threat of German invasion. But isolationist rhetoric ran high in the United States, leaving little appetite to provide assistance to Britain or Europe.

However, domestic U.S. opinion shifted in late 1940 and 1941 as Britain continued to hold out against German aggression, while Europe suffered under the weight of the Nazis. On 27 September 1940, Germany, Italy and Japan signed the Tripartite Pact, extending the reach of the Axis alliance through Asia. In late 1940, Roosevelt and his advisers devised a way to provide aid to Britain, Europe and Asia through the Lend-Lease Act. This enabled the U.S. government to help the Allied effort without directly involving the United States in the war. In his so-called 'fireside chat' radio address to the nation on 29 December 1940, President Roosevelt told the American people of his plan. In his speech, he outlined the need to ramp up production of military hardware and other vital supplies to help the Allies, which in turn would support the defence of the United States:

> We must be the great arsenal of democracy. For us this is an emergency as serious as war itself. We must apply ourselves to our task with the same resolution, the same sense of urgency, the same spirit of patriotism and sacrifice as we would show were we at war.[1]

The Lend-Lease bill was introduced into Congress on 19 January 1941. It sought to provide goods and services to support any country whose defence would in turn 'promote the defense of the United States'.[2] In essence, the measure was designed as a way to protect American interests and territories by providing munitions and other goods to the Allies, particularly Britain, to fight the Axis, while keeping the United States out of an active combat role.

Moving quickly through Congress, the bill was voted on and passed in the House of Representatives on 8 February 1941. The bill then moved to the Senate, where it was passed on 8 March. The final bill passed Congress three days later, with only minor revisions, by a vote of 317 to 71, and the president signed it that day.[3]

Once the bill was passed and mechanisms were put in place to facilitate the flow of Lend-Lease goods, the UK and Greece were the first to benefit from the legislation. Initial shipments to these two countries commenced in April 1941, which were largely comprised of food and industrial goods. As the defence industry in the United States geared up to meet demand, large shipments of military hardware, including weapons and military vehicles, were also sent.

That same year, China (in May) and Norway (in June) also began receiving Lend-Lease goods to support their war efforts. After Germany invaded the Soviet Union in June 1941, the USSR joined the Allied forces, and subsequently began receiving Lend-Lease aid in November. The following year, many other countries were added to the rolls of Lend-Lease recipients, including Australia and New Zealand and countries in Latin

People gathering to meet the first American food ship to arrive under Lend-Lease in Britain, 1941.

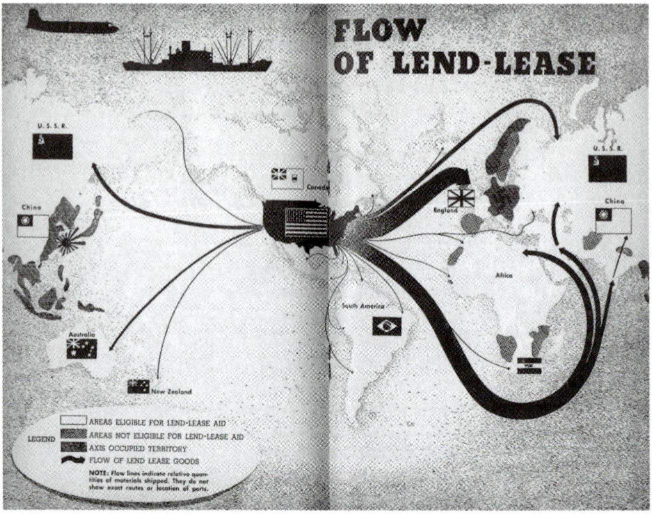

'Flow of Lend-Lease Goods', from Horace Taylor, *How Shall Lend-Lease Accounts Be Settled?* (1945).

America such as Chile, Brazil and Mexico. The United States spent billions of dollars on Lend-Lease, distributing materials according to need to these different areas of the world. Between March 1941 and June 1944, the United States shipped $21.5 billion to the Allied countries around the world.[4]

Overall, Lend-Lease accounted for approximately 15 per cent of total U.S. war costs by June 1944.[5] More than half of the aid sent was in the form of munitions. But agricultural products comprised 12.9 per cent of all goods sent to the Allies by the summer of 1944. The highest amount of aid, $10.3 billion, went to the UK, Australia and New Zealand, illustrating the central role such aid played in supporting the war effort among these populations.[6]

Lend-Lease provided vital supplies to the Allied military and civilian fronts. This was particularly true with its food provisions. American food supplies enabled the war effort throughout the world to continue, warding off starvation and disease through the important comestibles that the country provided to the Allies. The Hormel Corporation played a crucial role in supplying protein in the form of SPAM and other meats to the Lend-Lease programme to sustain the Allies on all fronts. Although Jay Hormel had been opposed to any American intervention at the start of hostilities in Europe, he quickly changed course once the Lend-Lease bill was passed. His company became a major contributor to the Lend-Lease programme, gaining financially in the process.[7]

According to the Hormel company's official history, products produced and shipped overseas under Lend-Lease included SPAM, pork sausage and pork luncheon meat. These products were shipped in both 340-gram (12 oz) tins and bulk-sized tins.

Putting the U.S. government stamp on a carcass of inspected beef, Hormel plant, Austin, Minnesota, July 1941.

To save on tonnage and tin, the company also sent dehydrated pork shoulder, which was rehydrated and processed in overseas facilities.[8]

The prevalence of SPAM in Lend-Lease shipments meant that it became a ubiquitous food available to the Allies. Hormel, as well as other meat manufacturers, also produced a unique tinned luncheon meat akin to SPAM for the Soviet market known as 'Cvinaya Toshonka', which consisted of pork, salt, bay leaves, black pepper and onion. This food provided the calories needed for people in the USSR, who faced a lack of food supplies for much of the war. In total, the Soviet Union received approximately 3 million tonnes of food from the United States over the course of the Lend-Lease programme, and Cvinaya Toshonka constituted an important part of this food tonnage.[9] Hormel produced 450,000 kilograms (1 million lb) or 500 tonnes of the product in 800-gram (28 oz) tins.[10]

The USA Enters the War

The Lend-Lease agreement set the United States on the path of a war economy, swinging the manufacturing industry towards the production of goods to meet the Allies' needs, but it was the Japanese assault on Pearl Harbor on the morning of 7 December 1941 that marked the point of the country's entry into the Second World War. The surprise attack on the U.S. naval base in Hawaii pushed the nation into a total wartime economy. The shift to active war status created competing demands between the USA's obligations under Lend-Lease, its own military needs and supplies for the home front. The distribution of the limited supply of materials between these elements, however, was not on an equal footing. The Allies and the U.S. military were given preference over the domestic populace in terms of their

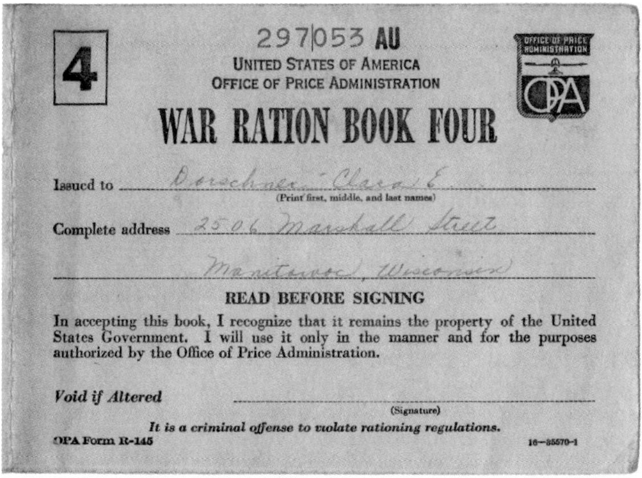

297|053 AU

UNITED STATES OF AMERICA
OFFICE OF PRICE ADMINISTRATION

4

WAR RATION BOOK FOUR

Issued to Dorschner, Clara E.
(Print first, middle, and last names)

Complete address 2506 Marshall Street
Manitowoc, Wisconsin

READ BEFORE SIGNING

In accepting this book, I recognize that it remains the property of the United States Government. I will use it only in the manner and for the purposes authorized by the Office of Price Administration.

Void if Altered ______________________ (Signature)

It is a criminal offense to violate rationing regulations.

OPA Form R-145 16—35570-1

U.S. war ration book, 1943.

requirements. Such inequalities and large demands for supplies necessitated that the U.S. government put in place a system of rationing for the domestic population, which limited essentials such as petrol, clothing and food. These restrictions did not apply to the U.S. service members or the Allies.

Moving swiftly on from the Congressional declaration of war on 11 December 1941, President Roosevelt set out the mechanisms for food rationing in January 1942 with the Emergency Price Control Act, giving the Office of Price Administration the power to begin preparations for the restrictions. In May of that same year, limited food rationing was rolled out with the control of sugar, followed by that of coffee. In the following year, rationed goods included processed foods, such as SPAM and other Hormel products, meat, cheese, butter, fats and jams. Some items such as fresh fruit and vegetables and cigarettes were never rationed. Consumers had to bring along their ration books to their local shops, where the attendants removed the appropriate stamps from the books for that week, which corresponded to the items that the customer wished to purchase. Consumers then paid for those items. The food controls were governed by two types of restrictions, depending on which category they fell into. Items such as coffee and sugar were allocated by a set amount for a certain period of time, so that consumers handed in their rationing stamps for a particular amount of food during a specific period. The amount of goods that people could purchase varied throughout the war according to supply levels. Other foods were placed on the red or blue points system, which corresponded to a certain number of stamps in the ration book. Items covered on red points included meat, some dairy products and fats. Foods that fell under the blue points included tinned foods, such as SPAM. Individuals were given six red stamps and five blue stamps per month, which were each worth ten points (sixty red points, fifty blue points) and which they used to obtain food on the points system. If a consumer did not use the total value of one stamp, or the ten points, when they purchased a product, the store would provide them with change in the form of red or blue tokens, each worth one point, depending on the type and amount of change needed.

The government set the points value for each item of food. The number of points needed for each of the goods on either

Office of Price Administration tokens from the Second World War.

blue or red points depended on supply and demand. It was each consumer's responsibility to determine how best to use their points to obtain the goods that they needed to sustain their consumption needs in wartime.

The U.S. government urged people to take up victory gardens to supplement the fresh fruit and vegetables available in the shops. As a result, back gardens, school playing fields, community parks and land that normally wasn't used in cultivation were turned into allotments to support the war effort. Researchers estimate that 20 million gardens of varying size and type were created and maintained throughout the United States to sustain the consumption needs of the country during the conflict.[11]

The U.S. government also recommended that families take advantage of the abundance of fresh produce in season by preserving them for the winter. Doing so enabled families to stretch their food supplies, which took some of the pressure off the rationing system. As part of the process, families could make an application to the U.S. Department of Agriculture for up to 9 kilograms (20 lb) of extra sugar beyond the rationed amount to aid in the preservation of the food.[12]

The rationing of sugar on the home front had a direct impact on the production of SPAM for the domestic population. Sugar is one of the key ingredients of SPAM, and so the sugar content had to be reduced in the domestic SPAM recipe to conform to the restrictions. Hormel records show that the company had to reduce its use of sugar by 20 per cent.[13] Regardless, the change in the recipe created neither a downturn in domestic demand nor a reduction in the production output at Hormel's manufacturing facilities. Demand for the product remained high in spite of this restriction. It was an inexpensive, convenient and well-recognized brand name, making it a popular choice for busy, war-weary housewives.

J. H. Burdett, *War Gardens for Victory: Grow Vitamins at Your Kitchen Door*, 1939–45, lithograph.

One of the other major impediments to domestic production of SPAM was the dearth of tin as the war progressed. Supplies of tin from Asia were cut off due to enemy occupation of islands in the Pacific and losses in the Atlantic due to German submarine action. Loss of supplies coupled with the demands for tin from the U.S. military, Allied militaries and Lend-Lease orders resulted in the rationing of tin on the U.S. home front. The limitations placed on the domestic use of metal by the government forced Hormel to restrict the number of tinned products that it could offer to the American market in wartime. Some popular lines of food were discontinued for the duration of the war, including Chicken a la King, Dinty Moore Beef Stew, canned bacon and its chilli con carne.[14] Instead, the company concentrated its domestic output on the production of select items, including luncheon meats and SPAM.[15]

While the home front was controlled by these limitations on food as part of total war, the U.S. military had no such restrictions. No limitations were placed on the amount of sugar or other foods furnished to the soldiers, sailors or airmen and airwomen. Nor did the Services face tin restrictions. Indeed, much of the food available, particularly the goods produced by Hormel, was provided to the military without the curbs on consumption faced by the U.S. home front.

Throughout the war, the U.S. military grew by an incredible amount, so that by its end more than 16 million women and men were actively serving in it.[16] The rapidly expanding military required huge amounts of food, both fresh and preserved, to fuel its efforts. As a result, Hormel became a major supplier to

A housewife receiving help from a grocer with her food shop, 1942.

the U.S. military of fresh and processed tinned meat, producing items such as SPAM, luncheon meat and corned beef hash for the military services. Hormel's diverse products could be found throughout the different types of food packs that the military provided to its personnel. One of the most prominent of these provisions was the K-ration: at the height of demand, Hormel produced products for 250,000 of these rations per day.[17] Developed during the Second World War, K-rations were ready-packed meals for individual soldiers to eat while in the field. As a set of three meals a day, it enabled soldiers to consume 2,800 total calories per day. The items in the three-meal set were tinned, dried or non-perishable to make them easily transportable and convenient for consumption. Hormel also provided many of its products in bulk quantities to military base mess halls. Although the amount and type of foods that Hormel supplied to the U.S. military varied, the majority of the millions of tins of food that the company produced throughout the war years went to the U.S. military and to Allies overseas. Before Lend-Lease and the American entry into the war in 1941, Hormel produced 70 per cent of its products for the civilian market and 30 per cent for the military.[18] However, the official company history states that by 1944 it provided up to 90 per cent of its products to the U.S. government for the military and Lend-Lease recipients.[19] By February 1945, Hormel shifted its production again to provide more food to the U.S. domestic market, but the company was still providing 65 per cent of all of its manufactured goods to the U.S. government.[20]

The ubiquity of Hormel products coupled with the SPAM brand recognition meant that similar pork products, whether they were produced by Hormel or not, were almost universally called 'SPAM'. During the war, the U.S. military requested that Hormel and other companies produce a luncheon meat known as 'defense ham', a tinned pork product that was similar in texture and colour to SPAM but had a longer cure and heavier smoke to enable the food to endure the difficult conditions in battle zones. The vast majority of 'defense ham' that soldiers and sailors consumed during the war was sealed in 2.7-kilogram (6 lb) tins and shipped to soldiers for use in military mess halls. 'SPAM' was used as a generic noun to refer to this new food, despite the differences in processing and taste of the wartime product. Hormel, afraid of having negative stigma attached to its food through this general use of the name 'SPAM', sent out a survey in April 1943 to its former employees serving in the military to ascertain if service members were using 'SPAM' as a blanket term for all luncheon meat, and if so, why. Over the next few months, Hormel received response letters from its former employees demonstrating that there was a wide range of knowledge about and language practices by service members when using the term 'SPAM' as an all-encompassing word for any processed pork in a tin. Many members of the military were indeed calling all tinned meat 'SPAM', regardless of the food's actual origin, and as a result, opinions differed widely about the pork masquerading as 'SPAM', ranging from wonderful to less than desirable fare.[21]

Regardless of the level of quality, due to the pervasiveness and the monotony of eating copious amounts of luncheon meat, whether produced by Hormel or not, SPAM and processed pork products of a similar nature filled a vital need in wartime, not only for the U.S. military, but for Allied militaries and civilians. It is SPAM's notoriety, or perhaps its infamy, or a combination of both, which has made it an enduring symbol of American culture and foodways the world over, impacting the culinary history and cultural identities of millions of people.

Ration book and clothing coupon book issued to British civilians during the Second World War.

3
SPAM on the British Home Front

On land and at sea, the Second World War caused great disruptions to the international supply chain, which compounded the issue of food supply in the UK. Since the 1920s, Britain's agriculture had been in decline, and it was dependent on food imports from its empire, Commonwealth and trading partners, particularly the USA, to provide enough calories to feed its growing population. This pre-existing situation, coupled with German submarine action from the start of the war in September 1939, necessitated the introduction of food rationing in Britain by January 1940. However, food rationing would not end when hostilities concluded in 1945. Rather, British food rationing continued for another nine years until 1954, primarily as a consequence of the country's massive war debts.

The first goods to be rationed in the UK after petrol were bacon, ham, butter and sugar. Other goods such as meat, cheese, margarine and tea were added later to the list. Basic ration amounts varied depending on which category a person fell into. The categories were adult rations (buff-coloured ration book); pregnant women, nursing mothers and children under five (green ration book); and children between the ages of five and sixteen years of age (blue ration book). A set amount of rationed food was given per category to evenly and fairly distribute the food to the three groups. Each category was organized to ensure that individuals in these groups received the right amount of nutrition to maintain their health.

Members of the public took their ration books to the butcher, the green grocer and other stores at which the right type and amount of coupons were removed for a particular period of time according to each person's allotted amount of food. The customer then paid for their food. If patrons failed to bring their ration books with them, shop assistants were not legally allowed to sell them rationed food. However, in reality, under-the-counter sales in which shop owners or assistants gave individuals a little something extra 'off the ration' did occur in shops throughout the country. People also participated in illegal, black-market dealings by selling and buying stolen food at higher-than-usual prices, while not collecting ration stamps.[1]

In an effort to utilize goods in the shop, which weren't in large enough quantities to be guaranteed on the ration, but to enable their distribution and availability to the largest number of customers, the British government instituted the personal points system in 1942. Under this programme, individuals were given sixteen (later 24) points per month to spend on goods that were not on the basic ration but were controlled. These goods included rice, breakfast cereal and tinned foods, such as SPAM.

The amount, type and quality of the meat ration varied throughout this time, and many people's diets became significantly more vegetarian. Indeed, the Ministry of Food made a concerted effort through publicity campaigns on the radio, in newspapers and on film to urge people to consume more vegetables than meat for the bulk of their daily caloric intake.

Crucial to maintaining Britain's food rationing system, including the personal points allocation, was the influx of Lend-Lease goods from the United States. Over the course of the programme, the United States provided approximately 10 per

Queues formed by rationing and food shortages in wartime London, 1945.

cent of Britain's total wartime food supply, including eggs, cheese, bacon and the important protein source SPAM.[2] Such supplies supplemented the British domestic level of food, as well as goods that it could obtain through its empire, enabling the UK to provide a sufficient diet to its citizens and its military. From 1942 onwards, Hormel began shipping tinned goods to the Allies, the bulk of the supply going to Britain, which was holding out against Germany and German-occupied Europe.[3] The availability of this large amount of tinned meat, coupled with easy and inexpensive access compared with rationed meat, ensured that SPAM became a ubiquitous part of Britain's wartime landscape. However, reception of the food varied considerably.

Prior to the introduction of Lend-Lease goods from the United States, SPAM was a known quantity in the UK. Newforge Foods in Liverpool had contracted with Hormel Foods to make the product in the UK starting in 1941, but short supplies of meat and tin prevented the production of enough of the food to meet the need.[4] Thus the arrival of SPAM and other Hormel goods from America through the Lend-Lease programme was met by many with open arms. Hormel sent Britain 340-gram (12 oz) tins of SPAM, as well as 2.7-kilogram (6 lb) containers of luncheon meat.[5] Many in Britain hailed SPAM as a gift from the United States, benevolently bestowed on them by its leader, President Franklin D. Roosevelt. Such praise was even set to verse, as is evident in an adaptation of a Robert Burns poem that appeared in the *Sunday Post* on 28 March 1943. The poem highlights how SPAM constituted an important part of the civilian war workers' diet and the value that people placed on having the tinned good. While Lord Woolton, Britain's second minister of food, is acknowledged in the poem for keeping the country going on rations, it was SPAM and, by association, the United States that garnered praise from workers.

The availability of this preserved meat in steady supply on the new UK system of personal points provided relief to overtaxed housewives and added variety to their diet. The contents of the tin were viewed by some as symbolic of the American lifestyle, bringing a taste of something different, and even a touch of the exotic into the drab lives of the war-weary British. Referring to SPAM as a one of the 'trans-Atlantic delicacies' in 1942, the British newspaper the *Rochdale Observer* urged readers to break out of their conservative eating habits based on traditional British fare, and try something new. The paper also suggested that SPAM was a product connected with the glitz of American culture, to which the youth of Britain would be well disposed:

> Perhaps we should do better to leave our shopping to the young, who would instinctively be attracted to SPAM – it sounds so much like Scram that its purchase would

seem to make them sharers in the high, hot-dog life of Hollywood, and the traditional 'Co-op. Shop' would take on the glamour of El Morocco.[6]

Purchasing SPAM was not simply a matter of using personal points wisely; it was the act of buying into the American way of life. In obtaining and then consuming SPAM, individuals were creating links between their consumption habits and their

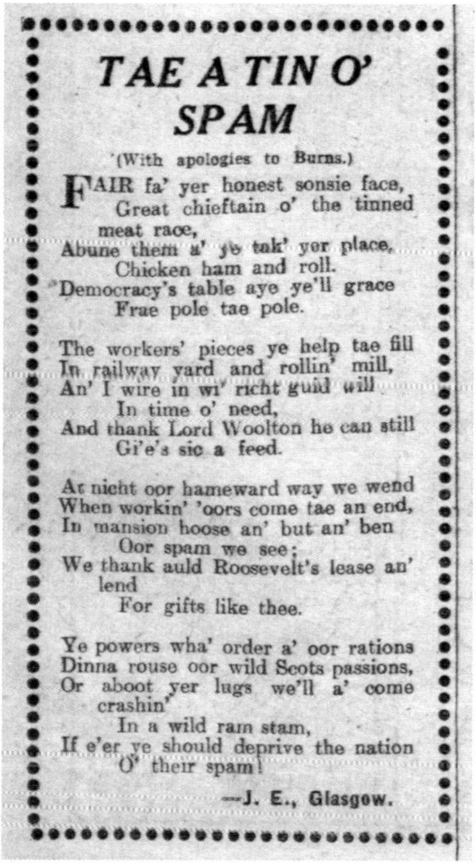

TAE A TIN O' SPAM

(With apologies to Burns.)

FAIR fa' yer honest sonsie face,
Great chieftain o' the tinned meat race,
Abune them a' ye tak' yer place,
Chicken ham and roll.
Democracy's table aye ye'll grace
Frae pole tae pole.

The workers' pieces ye help tae fill
In railway yard and rollin' mill,
An' I wire in wi' richt guid will
In time o' need,
And thank Lord Woolton he can still
Gi'e's sic a feed.

At nicht oor hameward way we wend
When workin' 'oors come tae an end,
In mansion hoose an' but an' ben
Oor spam we see;
We thank auld Roosevelt's lease an' lend
For gifts like thee.

Ye powers wha' order a' oor rations
Dinna rouse oor wild Scots passions,
Or aboot yer lugs we'll a' come crashin'
In a wild ram stam,
If e'er ye should deprive the nation
O' their spam!

—J. E., Glasgow.

Robert Burns's poetry adapted in praise of President Roosevelt: 'Tae a Tin o' SPAM', *Sunday Post*, 28 March 1943.

American cousins across the Atlantic, enabling them to imagine themselves participating in the glamorous lifestyle projected on cinema screens across Britain. Buying the food also offered some agency to the British to counter their own drab and difficult wartime existence.

The UK's ability to consume SPAM and other food from the United States rested on the capability of the British Navy and Merchant Navy to transport these goods. Many local governments worked to show their appreciation for the naval branches of the military by holding fundraising events. In many towns, newspapers advertised fundraising campaigns, and municipal groups sponsored competitions and put on different events to obtain donations. In its advertisement for Warship Week in 1942 and its bid to raise money to help build a new corvette, the War Savings Committee of the Borough of Heston and Isleworth reminded people, 'So when you folk go chasing Prem, Mor, SPAM and such-like trans-Atlantic luxuries, just think of the great little ships that brought them safely here.'[7] In Hartlepool, Warship Week was heralded by a poem written by the local greengrocer, W. M. Robertson:

> We've had SPAM, treet, and more,
> Ships, guns, food galore,
> From the Great USA overseas, Canada, the Cape,
> and Australia, too.
> Our troubles have helped to appease.
> Have you thought, who has brought
> All this stuff many miles
> To our shores, through the enemy lines?
> But what of the cost?
> Fine ships have been sunk, many brave hearts
> Were lost.
> They gave us their best,

They stood up to the test.
If their sacrifice you would repay, Lend to Defend,
  Don't on others depend.
Give your ALL; Yes, and GIVE IT TO-DAY.[8]

The poem reminds the home front that their ability to consume SPAM and other goods from the United States as part of their wartime diet was dependent on the work of the Navy and Merchant Navy. The piece warned that to sustain their food security, people needed to show their generosity for the cause.

Despite positive representations of SPAM in the British press, there were many detractors, including those who grew tired of consuming SPAM on a regular or even daily basis due to the meat ration and the ease of availability and affordability of the tinned food on personal points. To help make SPAM more palatable, the newspapers were full of recipes and helpful hints on how to insert SPAM into traditional British dishes in place of other meat. Recipes were offered for dishes such as SPAM fritters, all manner of SPAM and egg combinations, and even one for tripe and SPAM pie.[9] Such recipes were invariably aimed at women, who did the majority of household cooking chores. Historically in Britain, women have been held responsible for obtaining food and producing meals for their families, and thus the British government made a concerted effort to lean into these stereotypical gendered expectations of model domestic women, particularly married women, to ensure that the nation was well fed. Indeed, officials promoted women's work in the kitchen as a woman's primary and most vital contribution to the war effort, above other war work that the individual might undertake.[10] Throughout the conflict, women were bombarded with a slew of tips, techniques and recommendations on how to make the most of their rations and personal points, and particularly how to use SPAM to make appealing meals.

Magazines offered women advice on how to integrate the tinned meat into their family's daily diet in creative ways. The Italian-sounding recipe name 'Escaloppe Amigoni' from a 1942 issue of the weekly journal *The Sketch* adds a touch of sophistication to what is essentially battered and fried SPAM with sautéed vegetables. In the domestic setting, the onslaught of SPAM and the persistent promotion of women's work as fulfillment of ideal domesticity through their cookery practices was met with dislike and distaste by many as the war dragged on.

The monotony of meals, particularly those containing SPAM, is epitomized by a cartoon published in the *Sunday Post* in March 1944. Depicted is a lioness seeking to fulfil the expectations of wartime femininity by providing a meal for her family, which she constructs with the consumables available to her.

EVERY WOMAN'S RECIPES.

A SUBSTITUTE FOR SWEET CORN SUITABLE FOR HORS D'ŒUVRE.

2 oz. pearl barley.
1 cupful of Oxo.
1 oz. margarine.
1 dessertspoonful flour.
1 cupful of milk.

Put 2 oz. of pearl barley into a saucepan with one large cupful of Oxo (one cube diluted in water). Leave it simmering gently until all the liquid has been absorbed. When cold, mix the barley with a white sauce made of 1 oz. of margarine, one dessertspoonful of flour and one cup of milk. Serve it hot or cold as preferred.

ESCALOPPE AMIGONI.

Spam.
Flour.
Milk.
Breadcrumbs.
Six carrots.
Two onions.
One turnip.
Margarine.
Potatoes.

Cut the required number of slices, about ¼ in. thick, from a roll of tinned Spam; roll them in flour, dip them into milk and cover them thickly with breadcrumbs. Meanwhile slice up half a dozen large carrots, well washed and scraped, two large onions, and one turnip. Put the mixed vegetables into sufficient margarine or other fat to cover them and leave on a slow fire for twenty minutes or until tender. Fry the Spam in plenty of boiling fat over a quick fire until nicely browned all over. Arrange the vegetables in circular mounds on a dish, place the escaloppes on them, and serve with mashed potatoes.

Magazine feature for wartime recipes, including a method for using SPAM to make 'Escaloppe Amigoni', from *The Sketch*, 8 April 1942.

'Sorry, dear, but it's – er – sausages and SPAM again', *Sunday Post*, 19 March 1944.

Housewives' use of SPAM in multiple, varied and frequent ways aligned with government recommendations and media representations. However, as the lion's demeanour suggests in the cartoon, such efforts were not always welcome or appreciated in the home, particularly when they revolved around SPAM.

As in the U.S. military, 'SPAM' became the catch-all term in the UK for any pork luncheon meat regardless of whether it was actual SPAM or not, and whether it was manufactured by Hormel or a rival company.[11] The overabundance and easy access to the pork product, coupled with the use of the term 'SPAM' in a general sense, irrespective of the actual producer, compounded the issue of discontent directed at the food in many households.

The SPAM sandwich was a go-to meal for many housewives. This type of meal predominated in wartime, presenting an adaptation of a traditional British sandwich filled with some type of meat such as pork, which was the quickest meal for busy housewives to prepare. However, the continued use of SPAM in sandwiches became, for some, a monotonous undertaking, as epitomized in this poem:

> Housewives complain of being tired of sandwiches
> and want something to replace them.
> Picnic days in halcyon past
> Supper snacks at the ball,
> Many a hasty light repast
> The sandwich doth recall
> We got it thin, we got it thick,
> And if a trifle stale.
> It ever could be washed down quick
> With champagne or with ale.
> Seductive, it on a sideboard lay
> At hunger's beck and call,
> And stuck its post for many a day
> Upon the railway stall.
> In war-time it has proved a friend,
> Though gone the days of ham,
> We've got along with lease and lend
> of Bully Beef and Spam.
> So, housewives, cut out, sandwich hate,
> and when you're saying grace,
> Just ask for yet another plate.
> The last one to replace.[12]

Although it was a meal that connected with British foodways, it did not follow that it was always a welcome substitute for pre-war food. But the poem's author implies that women should be grateful and thankful for SPAM and other such foods, as it enables them to feed their families in wartime.

The ease with which SPAM could be made into a sandwich and the abundance of supply ensured that it was one of the most common foods provided to the populace in wartime catering facilities. Public sites of consumption such as work canteens, British Restaurants – kitchens set up during the Second World War to feed those unhoused by bombing or struggling to feed themselves under the ration system, among other reasons – and cafés regularly featured SPAM sandwiches and other SPAM dishes on their menus as an inexpensive way to feed the masses and stretch resources. The dining establishments provided inexpensive, filling and nutritious meals that did not require diners to forfeit their ration coupons. The restaurants also served as a useful way to take the pressure off housewives to organize family

Members of the public enjoying a meal in one of the British Restaurants established during the Second World War, London, 1943.

rations and cook all meals, enabling family members to eat away from home and off the ration.[13] But there was a backlash in the public and in the newspapers against what people viewed as the overuse of SPAM in these settings. At a meeting of British Restaurant organizers and caterers, the *West Sussex Gazette* reported that 'members look forward to the time when they may be able to place pre-war menus before a SPAM-weary world.'[14] To combat such negative views of SPAM and encourage people to continue eating it in dining facilities, various newspapers suggested using Continental names for SPAM dishes to invest unappealing wartime meals with a sense of the exotic.

In one Soho restaurant, SPAM's appearance on the menu was dubbed 'Escalope du Barry', after the glamorous French courtesan and mistress of King Louis XV the Comtesse du Barry. The dish's listing on the menu was accompanied by a poem written by Bertha Jordan, which appeared on 8 January 1943 in the *Liverpool Echo*:

> This glamour title will invest
> SPAM with allure, increase demand:
> Madame, we knew, was often pressed.
> We trust the lady was not canned![15]

Although corny in nature, this poem reiterates the need to make SPAM more appealing through wordplay. Since restaurants had few options in terms of food supply, using foreign titles enabled them to control the name, at least, if not the taste of dishes made with SPAM. One wonders if such actions had a positive impact on people's perception of the food, which seems doubtful.

SPAM served as a useful protein substitute for traditional British fare of meat, including lamb and pork. However, many people in society drew a gendered line around SPAM. Meat has been traditionally viewed as men's food, and often in homes, particularly the British working-class households of the Victorian period onwards, meat was distributed unevenly among family members, with men taking the largest portion of the protein.[16] These stereotypical consumption practices continued into the war. Indeed, when the British government set the same basic level of meat ration for all segments of the adult population regardless of occupation, it was workers in heavy industry, which consisted primarily of working-class men, who

François-Hubert Drouais, *Jeanne Bécu, Comtesse du Barry*, c. 1770–74, oil on canvas.

objected to the change in their pre-war consumption habits, which relied heavily on meat intake, and viewed the level set by the government as inadequate for their needs. The voices of dissent among the labour force pushed the government to institute an additional meat ration for these workers through their work canteens.[17] Eating meals at these sites often offered the men a respite from the bombardment of SPAM, particularly SPAM sandwiches, enabling them to obtain extra meat unavailable in the home. One newspaper report from the Sunderland shipping yard illustrates the men's discontent with the meals their wives could provide, which consisted primarily of SPAM sandwiches. It illustrates how they hoped to be able to access the extra meat allocated in the work canteens, rather than be forced to rely on inferior SPAM sandwiches from home.[18] This set up a gender divide between housewives' access to SPAM in order to make sandwiches, and the extra meat apportioned to the male workers in heavy industry. SPAM was firmly in the domestic setting as the inferior meat, while the traditional male sphere of work had access to traditional forms of meat.

Elsewhere in public eating venues, access to meat-based dishes took on gendered connotations, perpetuating the belief that meat, if in short supply, should be reserved for men. An article in the *Shields Daily News* in 1943 demonstrated the gender divide around food.[19] A female war worker went to her local café and requested a meat pie, but was told that she could not have one. The meat pies, she was told, were reserved for men's lunches. Instead, the waiter offered her a SPAM sandwich. This report suggests a wartime protein hierarchy. Men, whatever their occupation, were prioritized to receive the larger portion of meat. However, the alternative meat, SPAM, which was viewed as less valuable, was given to women, whose work, this story suggests, was seen as less significant to the war effort. SPAM then was perceived by society as a substitute and inferior food, suitable for women's needs but not sustaining enough for men's requirements.

In the final years of the war, the British public looked forward to the end of the conflict and their heavy reliance on SPAM. News articles raised the hope that after the war, eating habits could expand and take on more variety. A 1944 column in the *Daily Record* urged people to dream of tomorrow's better food horizons, while eating the wartime necessity of SPAM and eggs.[20]

The columnist envisioned a world in which SPAM would not be a component of most British dishes. The shift from wartime dependence on the tinned meat to more diverse dishes was ultimately placed on the shoulders of British housewives. Just as they had been advised by the government and the media on how to integrate SPAM into their wartime meals, women were told by these same sources that it was their responsibility to forgo these wartime measures when the conflict was over,

SPAM on the shelf of a UK grocery shop.

and to serve their returning husbands meals fit for their needs and wants – meals that did not include SPAM.

After the Second World War, British people's perspective on SPAM changed; to many, the food became a joke. SPAM was, for much of British society, something to be avoided, if possible. It became regarded as a lower-middle-class and working-class food that only people with less money would consume. Although SPAM is no longer produced in the UK, it is still available for purchase in the country's supermarkets, but it does not enjoy the same prevalence in British homes that it did during the war. SPAM can still be bought in some fish and chip shops in the form of SPAM fritters, reinforcing the view that it is a cheap and inexpensive meat. Hormel sells an extended line of SPAM products in the UK to cater to British tastes, which builds on and expands the wartime eating patterns of the British home front. Classic SPAM is available, along with SPAM Lite, SPAM with Real Bacon and, in the frozen aisle, SPAM Fritters and SPAM Cheesy Fritters. The SPAM varieties and sizes echo wartime shipments of the tinned pork under Lend-Lease. The 1.8-kilogram (4 lb) oblong tin, known today in the UK as the 'Catering Pack', is the same shape, but about half the size of the 27-kilogram (6 lb) oblong tins of pork luncheon meat that Hormel sent to Britain in the war. The frozen fritters represent the inventive means of breading and frying SPAM in the war, continuing the tradition today.

Product sales continue to grow, suggesting that SPAM still has a steady following of consumers and is finding ways to appeal to new customers. Every year, there is an unofficial marking of SPAM's continued presence in the UK with SPAM Appreciation Week, which falls in early March.[21] Its primary characteristics of being shelf-stable, reliable and inexpensive became important factors in creating huge, renewed demand for the tinned meat during the 2020–23 COVID-19 pandemic. When meat was in short supply and consumers sought to reduce their trips to the supermarket to limit the possibility of exposure to the virus, SPAM filled the void.

Although the wartime staple has fallen out of everyday use for many in Britain, its lasting presence on shop shelves symbolizes its enduring legacy. Its usefulness in times of national emergency ensures that it will remain a part of the UK's food traditions now and into the future.

The burning of USS *West Virginia* during the attack on Pearl Harbor, 7 December 1941.

4
SPAM in the Pacific

Japan's surprise attack on the U.S. military base at Pearl Harbor on 7 December 1941 threw the U.S. Pacific fleet into disarray, enabling the Japanese to quickly capture and then occupy the U.S. territories of Guam and Wake Island, severing America's ties to some of its vital, strategic positions in the area. The Japanese went on to capture additional assets in the region, occupying important American bases in the Philippines and the Marshall Islands. Many people living in these Japanese-occupied areas suffered horribly from hunger and forced labour.

Other islands in the Pacific, such as Midway Island and Samoa, served as vital sites for the USA's defence of the region. In these locations, the United States expanded its military presence, building military facilities and air strips from which Allied sorties could be launched against Japanese targets. Pearl Harbor also continued to serve as a crucial base for American operations throughout the war.

Wherever the U.S. military went, SPAM was sure to follow. 'Defense ham', or some version of pork luncheon meat, was served to American soldiers throughout the Pacific, just as it was dished up throughout the Atlantic theatre. SPAM and other Hormel products functioned as important military provisions that were easily packed and moved. Hormel products were served in mess halls and carried with soldiers across the Pacific

Receiving supplies in Guam, July 1944.

in the various military ration packs, such as the C-ration and the K-ration. Luncheon meat also formed a crucial part of the food aid provided by the American military to starving local populations in reclaimed territories. Individual tins of SPAM and other foodstuffs served as a ready supply of protein to liberated people. It was shelf-stable, accessible and easily transportable. The processed meat did not require any cooking facilities, as it was already cooked in a tin as part of the manufacturing process.

All of these attributes made SPAM and other tinned meats ideal provisions on the islands of the Pacific, which were decimated by the fighting. When the U.S. military recaptured Guam in August 1944, the local population, known as Chamorros, were given food by the military until the end of the war. One of the main sources of this food was SPAM. The processed food became so prevalent throughout the island that it became known as 'Chamorro steak'.[1]

The military's dominant role in places like Guam did not come without its pitfalls. Guam served as an important site of military activity and a vital staging ground for attacks on Japanese-held islands in the Pacific. As a result, the island witnessed a huge construction boom for the development of

Naval supply depot on Guam, 1945.

military bases. Such activity came at a cost to the local population, whose land was often confiscated by the military for construction purposes, bulldozing over prime agricultural fields to make way for airstrips and other military needs.[2] The reduction of arable land, coupled with the availability of well-paid clerical, labour and construction jobs, caused a tremendous shift in the lives of the Chamorro people, away from traditional ways based on agricultural work, to office and other jobs.[3] This change caused a steep decline in the country's agricultural output, forcing it to import large quantities of food to feed its people, and making it dependent on military supplies of food. Such provisions, including SPAM and other food imports, were given freely in wartime and eaten by the Chamorros for the first time.[4]

The traditional diet of natural, unprocessed foods, lean protein and produce on Guam also underwent a huge transformation. No longer able to sustain themselves with local, agricultural products, the diet of the Chamorro people shifted to ingesting food imports laden with large quantities of sodium, sugar and processed ingredients. Many of these consumables were American tinned and sweetened foods. The wartime consumption shifts have had a long-term and lasting impact on the health of the island's population. Today, those living on the island have higher levels of obesity, heart disease, diabetes and other cardiovascular diseases, compared to the American mainland, stemming from the unhealthy eating habits that have been passed down from the war generation to their children and grandchildren.[5]

As the Americans advanced through the Pacific, they continued to regain ground that they had lost to the Japanese in 1941 and 1942. Following on from Guam, they were able to recapture the Philippines in early 1945. Coming ashore, the American military found the local population starving and malnourished. Food was scarce and needed to be rationed. Into the food void, the American military plied Filipinos with SPAM and other tinned goods to help sustain them. SPAM and other foods provided by the military served to counter the high level of food insecurity that the islanders had faced during Japanese occupation. As such, SPAM became a high-value commodity, prized for its high protein content and easy transportability. It

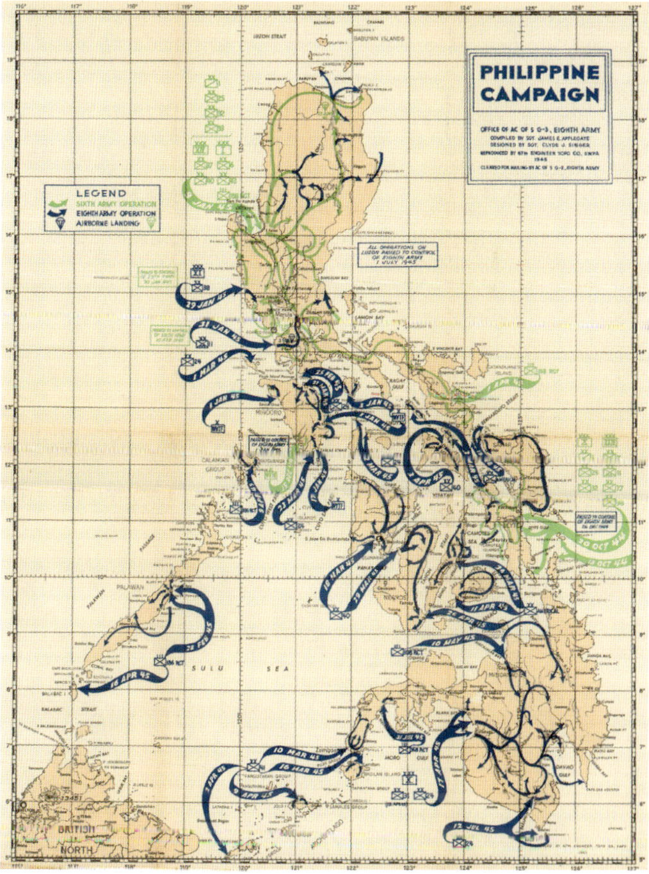

Map of the Philippines showing the U.S. military's major operations on the islands during the Second World War.

became synonymous with the American soldiers who freed the population from Japanese occupation, creating a positive association between U.S. culture and food that continues in the Philippines to this day. SPAM serves as a comfort food for Filipinos, a tradition that has passed down from generation to generation. But like the Chamorros of Guam, the indulgence in such food has caused a shift in Filipinos' consumption practices; the population's diet now includes large amounts of processed, salty and sugar-filled food imported from the USA. According to a 2023 study of U.S. export markets, the Philippines is the fifth-largest importer of America's processed food products globally, and the biggest overall in Southeast Asia.[6] The impact of the wartime diet has had and continues to have, as in Guam, a deleterious effect on many Filipinos' health, leading to higher levels of nutrition-related illnesses, including diabetes and heart

View of the naval operating base, Pearl Harbor, looking southwest, 30 October 1941.

disease, compared with earlier generations whose diet consisted largely of domestically grown, traditional food.

Prior to the start of the Second World War, Hawaii was an important military base and served as the hub of U.S. Naval activity in the Pacific. But following the loss of the Philippines and Guam to the Japanese, its vital position, coupled with its central role in military activities in the Pacific, created a boom in the number of personnel and military facilities in the territory. The U.S. Army alone witnessed an explosion in the number of servicemembers who were based in Hawaii at the time. According to the National WWII Museum, based in New Orleans, before the war an average of 15,000 army soldiers were based on the islands. But shortly after the attack on Pearl Harbor, 10,000 people were added to that number, nearly double the size of the force.[7] These numbers would continue to grow and fluctuate throughout the war.

The enormous expansion of the military on Hawaii had a tremendous impact on the landscape, economy and consumption practices of the islanders. The push to build military facilities created a large demand for labour, offering native Hawaiians steady work in the construction sector, and moving some away from traditional employment in industries such as agriculture and fishing. The military also put limits on fishing activities due to ongoing military exercises and preparations, shifting local diets away from lean meats such as fish and fresh produce. As with other sites of military activity in the Pacific, U.S. forces brought SPAM with them. Servicemembers' large presence spread the consumption of the tinned good throughout the local population. And, as elsewhere in the Pacific, the change in consumption patterns due to the military's presence enabled SPAM to step into the void, providing a ready, affordable and shelf-stable good that Hawaiians could insert into local dishes to sustain themselves throughout the war.

View of landing operations on Okinawa, 4 April 1945.

The last major – and deadliest – battle of the war in the Pacific occurred in the spring of 1945, when the Americans captured Okinawa, Japan. The island was in a coveted position in close proximity to the Japanese home islands, and it acted as a staging ground for the U.S. preparations to invade the Japanese mainland. As part of its occupation, the U.S. military provided food rations to the people of Okinawa. SPAM and similar luncheon meat played a central role in these provisions, providing the islanders with a taste of the processed pork for the first time and subsequently becoming enmeshed in the foodways of the island.[8] The acquisition and consumption of this food served not only as a marker of the war, but more broadly of the spread of American culture across the Pacific.

In the Pacific today, SPAM continues to enjoy a wide following of people who inherited their love of the food from their parents and grandparents. These people have also been influenced by the continued presence of the American military across the region. Guam is the world leader in SPAM consumption per person. With a population of 170,534 people, the average consumer eats around sixteen tins of the processed pork product yearly.[9] In the six McDonald's open on the island, SPAM is readily available and incorporated into the various offerings, such as SPAM, eggs and rice. McDonald's customers can also have a side dish of SPAM with classic menu items such as a cheeseburger and fries. The company goes through approximately four hundred cases of SPAM a month, 57,600 tins per year, to satisfy the demands of hungry SPAM enthusiasts on the island.[10]

Owing to the high demand for SPAM in Guam, the Hormel Corporation has tailor-made products suited specifically to the Guamanian market. SPAM Hot & Spicy with Tabasco was made as a way to link two popular products on the island, SPAM and Tabasco, which were introduced by American soldiers in the Second World War. In honour of the sixtieth anniversary of the liberation of Guam in 2004, the company also produced limited-edition SPAM tins with liberation labels.

The popularity of SPAM makes it a standard item in most Guamanian household pantries, and the food often gets infused into everyday and traditional dishes. One of the most common Guamanian dishes, *kelaguen*, is often made with SPAM. SPAM is chopped and lightly fried, and then mixed with lemon juice, onions and pieces of coconut. It can be eaten as a side dish or a main course.

Another popular recipe that incorporates the processed food is SPAM fried rice, or SPAM, fried rice and eggs. It is a simple and straightforward dish combining SPAM and rice, with the option of an egg, and fried in soy sauce. The dish is versatile and can be made with a wide variety of other ingredients.

The Second World War's long reach has also left its mark on Filipinos' consumption of SPAM. Considered a comfort food by

SPAM Hot & Spicy.

many families, it is widely eaten throughout the nation and is readily available in grocery shops. Indeed, after Guam and South Korea, the Philippines has one of the highest consumption rates of SPAM in the world, with millions of kilograms of the processed food eaten each year. The huge demand for SPAM and other Hormel products in the country led the Hormel Corporation, in 1999, to form its largest joint venture – this was with Pure Food Corporation, which is based in the Philippines. In 2001 Pure Food Corporation was bought by San Miguel Corporation, the largest food company in the Philippines, which continues to produce SPAM.

Ever keen to cater to consumers' taste preferences, Hormel developed SPAM with 'tocino' for the Filipino market in 2014. The Spanish word *tocino* means 'bacon' in English. Tocino is a common ingredient used in the recipes of many of the countries that were former colonies of the Spanish Empire, including in the Caribbean and the Philippines. SPAM with tocino is commonly made of pork belly, pork shoulder or pork ham, which is first cured, and then a sweetening agent, such as sugar, pineapple juice or orange juice, is added along with garlic and soy sauce. It can be found in the popular fried-rice dish *tosilog*. The ingredients of SPAM with Tocino reflect this melding of culinary traditions. The Filipino-inspired SPAM with Tocino consists of pork with ham, sugar, water, modified potato starch, salt, sodium phosphates, flavouring, spice, oleoresin of paprika and sodium nitrite.

Home cooks in the Philippines use SPAM with Tocino instead of bacon in traditional recipes for *tosilog* to produce the hybrid Spamsilog. This is a popular breakfast dish that blends SPAM with Tocino with sinangag (fried rice) and itlog (fried egg).

On Okinawa today, there is still a large U.S. military presence and an interrelated huge appetite for SPAM. In Japan, 7.2 million

Kelaguen with titiyas.

tins of the processed pork are sold annually, and on average, one tin is eaten per person, per week, most of it in Okinawa.[11] It is estimated that around 90 per cent of all SPAM imported to Japan is brought to Okinawa for consumption, symbolizing the enduring legacy of the war and the U.S. military, and the impact of American consumption patterns on Okinawans.[12]

Since 1969, Hormel has had a corporate presence on Okinawa. In that year, Okinawa Hormel Ltd. was established and continues to exist today, making it the organization's longest-standing joint venture. Through this agreement, the Okinawa arm of the Hormel corporation produces, markets and distributes a wide range of the company's products, including SPAM, Dinty Moore Beef Stew and Mary Kitchen® Corned Beef Hash.[13] Hormel even created a Japanese mascot, Spammy-kun,

SPAM with Tocino.

Spamsilog, the classic Filipino breakfast.

which is an anthropomorphized tin of SPAM that epitomizes the popularity of the brand.

National and international fast-food chains in the Pacific countries have also incorporated SPAM on to their menus to attract customers. In Japan, Burger King has introduced SPAM to its menu to draw on customers' interest in the tinned product. In 2011 the chain also offered mini SPAM sliders, marketing them to women as a smaller alternative to a large burger, suggesting a gendered association with the pork product versus a beef burger.[14] On Okinawa, the local fast-food chain Jef sells a *goya*, or bitter melon, burger with a slice of SPAM.[15] Domestic cooking in Japan, and particularly Okinawa, also utilizes SPAM. The postwar version of the traditional Okinawan dish *chanpurū* incorporates SPAM in its list of ingredients. The original dish usually includes tofu, meat, or fish as the main protein.

SPAM can at the SPAM Museum, Austin, Minnesota.

Today, the military presence in Hawaii has only grown and, with it, so has the consumption of SPAM. Hawaii now serves as the combatant command headquarters for the Indo-Pacific Command (U.S. INDOPACOM), overseeing U.S. military operations throughout the Pacific. The continued existence and reach of the military into Hawaiian culture, and the practice of eating SPAM, have had a lasting impact on the culinary patterns of native Hawaiians. The large influx of Asians, including Chamorro, Japanese, Koreans and Filipinos, to Hawaii has also helped to sustain and bolster the incorporation of SPAM into everyday dishes on the islands, and boosted sales figures. Hawaii is the USA's top consumer of SPAM, with the highest per capita rate of consumption per year. A total of 7 million tins of SPAM are sold each year on the islands, which equates to five tins of the food per person per year.[16]

SPAM varieties are sold in most major grocery stores and convenience stores such as 7-Eleven, and they feature on many restaurants' menus. The most prominent of these are McDonald's restaurants in Hawaii. Here SPAM is available on the menu throughout the day. The fast-food chain offers items such as the SPAM breakfast platter, which contains fried SPAM, eggs and rice.[17]

To compete with the popularity of the SPAM offerings of McDonald's in Hawaii, Burger King also offers SPAM on its menu. Customers can purchase a breakfast plate of spam, eggs and rice, as well as the Croissan'wich or Biscuit Sandwich, which contains SPAM.[18]

Hawaiian home cooks often keep a tin of SPAM at the ready and serve it as main fare. One of the most common uses of SPAM is in musubi, which is rice topped with a piece of SPAM and rolled in seaweed. This is also a popular dish in Japan.

These high levels of SPAM in everyday food practices do not come without a price. Today, the continually high levels of processed pork consumption by successive generations of Hawaiians potentially contributes negatively to the population's overall health and wellness. According to a study carried out jointly by researchers at the Centers for Disease Control and Prevention and the University of Hawaii, Honolulu, between 2018 and

Spam and egg musubi.

2022 Native Hawaiian and Pacific Islander adults had the second highest rate of cardiovascular disease and stroke in the United States. The study also found that these groups had a 7 per cent higher rate of death from these diseases.[19] Regardless, SPAM is loved and enjoyed throughout the Hawaiian islands.

5
SPAM and the Korean War

The end of the Second World War created new divisions and expanded political tensions around the world, particularly between the United States and the Soviet Union. As part of the settlement with Japan, and the road to post-war peace and reconstruction, the United States occupied the Korean peninsula from the 38th parallel downwards, while the USSR occupied it from the 38th parallel up to the border with China. This action was meant to be a temporary measure to stabilize and bring order to Korea after Japanese colonization, which had occurred from 1910 until 1945. However, Korea became the staging ground for the deepening Cold War between the two competing superpowers, the United States and the Soviet Union.

By 1948 the two superpowers had helped to set up two sovereign states. In the north, the Democratic People's Republic of Korea became a communist, totalitarian regime, under the leadership of Kim Il Sung, aligning itself with the Soviet Union and what would, in 1949, become the People's Republic of China. In the south, the Republic of Korea was established as a capitalist country tied to the Western world, particularly the United States. The political tensions at the border between the two states resulted in cross-border attacks. The mounting political and military pressure between the two halves of the peninsula culminated in North Korea's invasion of South Korea on 25 June 1950.

On the North Korean side, the Soviet Union helped to supply arms, vehicles and other forms of military support. Later, China would enter the war as a North Korean ally, supplying soldiers and munitions. The United Nations supported South Korea's war effort, with 21 member countries contributing aid and military personnel. Although the United States never formally declared war on North Korea, it provided the highest number of soldiers to the war, contributing 90 per cent of UN forces involved in the conflict.[1]

Throughout the war, the battle lines were shifting constantly. At times, the North penetrated deep into South Korean territory, while at other times soldiers from the South reached far into North Korea, almost to the Chinese border. Although this conflict was relatively short in comparison with the Second

A young Korean War refugee, carrying her brother, trudges past a Patton tank, Haengju, Korea, 9 June 1951.

North Korean refugees fleeing to the South, 1951.

World War, it resulted in utter devastation on the peninsula. The great upheaval of war and the continually shifting areas of active military operations across the two Koreas posed an ongoing threat of injury and death to civilians, leading to massive disruptions in the population, with more than 1.5 million North Koreans estimated to have fled to the South.[2]

The utter disruption to daily life resulted in massive gaps in supply lines and agricultural output, leading to severe shortages of food and other necessary goods to sustain life. Koreans in both countries faced unremitting hunger and starvation in the turmoil of war. Meat and other forms of protein were in particularly short supply, leaving people desperately trying to obtain enough calories to keep themselves and their families alive.

The war was finally halted in July 1953, when an armistice agreement was signed by leaders on both sides. Of the 1,636,970

U.S. service members (men and women) who served in the Korean War, 33,686 were killed and 103,284 were wounded.[3] More than 415,000 South Korean soldiers and over 600,000 North Korean soldiers were killed, and more than a million civilians on either side are estimated to have died, been wounded or gone missing during the conflict.[4]

As in the Second World War, the arrival of American soldiers to the zone of conflict meant the arrival of SPAM – millions of tins of it.[5] Hormel provided the U.S. military with supplies of SPAM for soldiers' meals and SPAM was also deployed as a means to connect with the civilian population during the conflict. The soldiers gave tins of the congealed meat to Koreans for diverse purposes. In some cases, the food was provided to civilians as a gift. In other cases, the tins were used as a means to leverage Koreans' hunger for information about military positions of enemy combatants.[6]

For the Koreans, their starvation made them desperate to obtain any form of protein that would enable them to survive. Some Koreans recall how their hunger drove them to steal food from U.S. military installations to have something to fill the empty stomachs of their children.[7] Other stories illustrate the sale of food scraps, including bits of SPAM left over from U.S. military mess hall meals, which Koreans bought in bags at the gates of U.S. bases.[8] The result of such desolation was that Korean people were introduced to many American tinned and processed foods, including SPAM. Indeed, SPAM became a highly sought-after form of protein, when no other form of meat could be obtained on the Korean market. A tin of the processed pork represented a highly prized, portable and long-lasting food that could be carried across the peninsula – particularly useful when people were forced to flee from the enemy. For the Korean people, SPAM, in both scrap and tinned form, represented the utter devastation of the two Koreas and the peninsula's poverty, as well as a life-saving protein. SPAM also became synonymous with American soldiers, American lifestyle and America in general.

After the armistice was signed, the U.S. military continued to have a large presence in South Korea and established bases across the country as a means to deter further North Korean aggression. In the deepening Cold War, the USA's military bases in South Korea served as strategic positions from which to guard against Chinese or Soviet military action. The continued presence of the soldiers, sailors and air personnel also meant the influx of American goods, such as SPAM, to the Post Exchanges, also known as 'PX' stores, on these bases. These shops were exclusive to American service personnel and their spouses, as Hormel did not have a licence to sell SPAM to the civilian population in South Korea. However, although SPAM was sold in the PX stores officially only to Americans, unofficially it was bought or smuggled out of military stores and sold on the Korean black market at an inflated price. While some people equated SPAM with the destruction of the war, many viewed the food as a rare and valuable commodity, which only wealthy Koreans could afford to purchase through illegal means.[9] Such post-war conditions continued to make the processed meat a much sought-after and highly prized, if expensive, food.

It remained a rare treat for most Koreans for the next several decades. Through the 1950s, South Korea struggled to emerge from the severe devastation of the war and to propel its economy forwards. The United States sent huge amounts of financial aid to prop up the economy, which was plagued by slow growth and corruption. Between 1946 and 1976, the United States made $12.6 billion available to the South Korean economy in an effort to shore up and support its growth.[10] Korean entrepreneurs and engineers, who were often educated in the United States, set up new companies or expanded existing ones that were often family-owned and operated: Corporations such as LG (1958), Hyundai (1967) and Samsung Electronics (1969) were created during this period. Such spurs of business creation and economic activity helped South Korea pull itself out of poverty and make huge gains in the world economy.[11]

Just after the war in August 1953, the Samsung Group, which started as a family-owned grocery company in 1938, launched CheilJedang Co., Ltd. It became Samsung's first manufacturing company, and Korea's first producer of processed sugar. The company's name itself means 'first sugar' in Korean. Later changing its name to CJ Cheiljedang, the company is now a well-known producer of many Korean branded food products, as well as a firm that has interests and major holdings in pharmaceuticals, the entertainment industry, home shopping and logistics. The company's interconnectivity with Samsung and its favourable position in the market enabled it to approach the Hormel corporation in 1986 to set up a licence to produce and sell Hormel products. Based in Seoul, it was able to gain exclusive rights from Hormel to produce and sell SPAM in South Korea.

Mass production of the food began in 1987, making SPAM widely available in shops and affordable to the average South Korean person for the first time. For many living on the peninsula, they had not encountered or had the option of obtaining SPAM since the Korean War ended, a 34-year food gap in Koreans' collective consumption memory. For many, the food was a known, if slightly distant, memory tinged with war, starvation and the U.S. military; it was a valuable protein remembered for abating food insecurity. For the generations of people who came after the war, SPAM was a wholly unknown and unexperienced taste, and people welcomed the opportunity to buy it as a ready-made, inexpensive meat. Despite or because of SPAM's initial introduction to the Korean people as a war food, or due to its former, post-war status as a rare, American luxury food available only to the wealthy, there was pent-up consumer demand for the product, and initial sales of the food were brisk. In the first year, CJ Cheiljedang estimates that it sold 500 tonnes of SPAM, and in the following year 1,000 tonnes were sold.[12]

A 1987 CJ Cheiljedang advertisement for SPAM depicts a young Korean woman wearing a cowgirl outfit with a Stetson-like hat and a vest standing behind a tin of SPAM. In the background is a picture of the Statue of Liberty. This advertisement makes clear the food's link to the United States, despite it being manufactured in Korea, suggesting that the food is synonymous with American liberty and the freedom of the American West. Through this advert, the company perpetuated these stereotypical images and motifs of the United States to persuade consumers that if they bought and ate this product, they were buying a piece of American culture. Absent here is any reference to the food's connection to the Korean War or the hunger endured by Koreans because of it. The advert was not asking Koreans to reminisce about the past. Rather, it encouraged Koreans to buy into American ideals and acted as an example of gastrodiplomacy: the use of American soft power to dominate Korean culture through building customer demand for the branded food product. This reinforced the cyclical forms of power between the United States and South Korea, in which the former was the dominant partner in the two nations' relationship.

SPAM remained a high-selling and well-consumed food in South Korea throughout the 1980s and '90s. But the turn of the millennium marked an explosion of SPAM sales in Korea as it became one of the most popular gifts to give on the Korean national holidays of Chuseok (추석) and Seollal (설날). Both of these traditional holidays in Korean culture follow the lunar

Japchae, stir-fried sweet potato noodle dish.

calendar. The former is a celebration of the harvest, which falls in either September or October of every year. It is a time of year when families gather together – many travelling great distances to visit family members in their hometowns – to make offerings of food and drink to their ancestors in their homes and at family gravesites.

Women in the family make elaborate meals of traditional foods such as *japchae* (잡채), a stir-fried sweet potato noodle dish; *pajeon* (파전), fried, savoury pancakes; and *seongpyon* (송편), small, half-moon shaped rice cakes filled with a variety of sweet ingredients such as sesame seeds and red bean paste. Families dress in traditional Korean clothes known as *hanboks* and celebrate the season together.

Seollal occurs in January or February to mark the end of the year and the beginning of the new one. This is also a time for family members to come together, honour their ancestors and celebrate over elaborate meals. Part of the celebrations involve the exchange of small gifts of food or alcohol, or, in the case of Seollal, money for children. In the 2000s the act of giving and receiving SPAM during these two holidays became a prevalent practice between Korean family, friends and company employees.[13] Single tins of the food are given, but more often people purchase SPAM gift sets, which come in a range of sizes, types and prices. Some sets contain a variety of different types of SPAM, while other, more exclusive and expensive sets include several tins of SPAM with fancy cooking oil. Prices can

Pajeon, a Korean savoury pancake made with spring onions.

Songpyeon, half-moon-shaped rice cake.

range from $20 for simple sets of SPAM, to up to $100 for deluxe gift sets. CJ Cheiljedang actively promotes SPAM as a preferred gift for these two traditional Korean festivities. On its website, next to a picture of a limited-edition SPAM classic gift box set, the company advises consumers, 'SPAM is the best gift that everyone loves. Share all the happy moments with your loved ones together.'[14] These cheerful sentiments are accompanied by a promotional video showing people giving SPAM gift sets to their loved ones and eating SPAM and rice with their family members in domestic settings. A grandfather is also pictured bringing a gift set to his grandchildren, who are dressed in traditional hanboks. Such representations portray the intergenerational promotion and reach of SPAM, tying family members who lived through the war to younger members, who are generations removed from the direct experience of the peninsular's conflict. The image of a gift of SPAM in this generational context illustrates how ingrained SPAM is within Korean culture, customs and identity.[15] The popularity,

Traditional Korean clothing worn during Chuseok Festival, Seoul, 2012.

prevalence and cultural expectation of exchanging gift sets represents a significant part of CJ Cheiljedang's annual income from the processed meat. The company estimates that the sale of SPAM gift sets makes up 60 per cent of its yearly profits from the sale of the food.[16] These profits continue to rise, year in and year out.

The high demand for the product and an effort to keep family food costs down has also led to a bustling second-hand market for the online sale of SPAM in Korea. Two of the most popular online websites that focus on the resale of goods (including food), Karrot Market and Joonggonara, sell tins of the processed meat at a discounted rate.[17] Doing so, particularly during the two national holidays, enables families to maintain what has now become the cultural practice of giving SPAM, while spending less on the act of doing so. The ubiquitousness of SPAM and its connection to Korean national holidays suggests the high value that the food continues to enjoy on the peninsula and its importance to the culinary practices of Korea, some of which stem from the Korean War and the continued American influence there.

South Korea today has a mature economy, and is one of the more economically developed and globalized countries of the world. Food insecurity is a distant memory for the older generations, and many young South Koreans have never known want or been forced to cut back on their caloric intake due to a lack of supplies. While many people in the United States view SPAM as a secondary and less-desirable form of meat, SPAM holds a special significance for South Koreans that belies its relatively inexpensive and processed nature. No longer a food needed to prevent hunger and starvation, SPAM has become an integral part of Korean foodways, and with it, Korean identity. Indeed, South Korea has the highest rate of SPAM sales outside of the United States (as opposed to the highest per capita rate of

Kimchi fried rice, which often contains fried SPAM.

consumption in Guam). The company figures put the annual sale of SPAM at nearly $400 million.[18]

Domestic production is centred at the CJ Cheiljedang factory in South Chungcheong Province, also known as Chungnam, which is located south of Seoul, along the coast and on the southwestern part of the peninsula. Here, workers make SPAM for the Korean market, which uses a somewhat different recipe from the one produced by Hormel in the USA. To fit the Korean palette, the variety of SPAM that is produced in the country is slightly less salty than its original American variant. The pork product is sold in South Korea by CJ Cheiljedang in seven varieties: SPAM Classic, SPAM 25% Light, SPAM Chicken Breast, SPAM Single Classic, SPAM Single 25% Light, SPAM Single Chicken Breast and SPAM Gimbap Ham.

Koreans incorporate the processed meat into their culinary practices and consumption habits differently from the Americans. People in the United States often eat SPAM in sandwich form or fried. While Koreans also tend to fry SPAM, one of the most common ways to eat it is over white rice. In many Korean dishes, SPAM acts as an alternative meat source in traditional Korean recipes, which originally contained other forms of meat, most commonly pork. One example is kimchi bokum bap (김치볶음밥), which translates to 'kimchi fried rice'. 'Bokum' means 'stir-fried' and 'bap' means rice. To make the recipe with the processed meat, SPAM is fried with white rice along with kimchi, gochujang, sesame oil, 'kim or seaweed, and spring onions. Fried eggs are an optional topping. Traditionally, the dish would have included pork, or other meat, if available.

SPAM is also a popular ingredient in kimbap (김밥). Kimbap is a quick go-to meal, which is often taken on outings or picnics. SPAM kimbap (스팸 김밥) consists of rice layered with vegetables and strips of SPAM rolled up into sheets of seaweed and cut into circular pieces. Traditionally, kimbap contains meat, which can include tuna or bulgogi (marinated pork or beef), but there is also a vegetable-based version. SPAM was added when the tinned good became widely available in Korea.

SPAM can also be found in another classic Korean dish, kimchi *jjigae* (김치찌개). *Jjigae*, which means 'stew', is essentially a spicy stew served in a cast-iron bowl, which is cooked

Kimbap with pieces of SPAM, bought on an express train in South Korea.

directly over the flames of a stove. Traditionally made with pork shoulder or pork belly, SPAM is the perfect meat substitute in this dish. In addition, the dish contains kimchi, gochujang, sesame oil, tofu and spring onions. Through these recipes, Koreans meld classic dishes with their love of SPAM to build onto and connect with Korean tastes and food preferences, allowing SPAM to become an important part of the country's cookery practices.

The use of SPAM, specifically in the Korean War, also led to the creation of a completely new dish. But the dish corresponds to and builds on the Korean tradition of the hot pot, containing ingredients that conform to Korean tastes. During the conflict, South Koreans had to cobble together any food that they had available to them to feed their families. *Budae-jjigae* (부대찌개), which translates to 'army stew' because of its origins, was the result of Koreans' efforts to utilize the food that they could get from the the USA in the face of widespread food insecurity. SPAM is the central component of the dish. Other ingredients include ramen noodles, hot dog or other sausages, American cheddar cheese, tofu, mushrooms, onions, garlic, gochujang and gochugaru, or red pepper flakes.

Budae-jjigae is extremely popular in South Korea today. There are many restaurants in Seoul and throughout the country that are dedicated solely to serving *budae-jjigae* with a wide variety of ingredient variations. The *budae-jjigae* chain of restaurants, Nolboo (놀부), has more than 1,000 locations throughout South Korea. With its long list of ingredients, *budae-jjigae* is usually cooked and served in a large pot at the centre of the table. It is a dish that is meant to be consumed family-style by groups of people. Patrons can choose from different types of *budae-jjigae* on the menu, and a waiter or waitress brings the ingredients to the table. Customers then sit around the large pot as ingredients are added and the dish cooks in front of

Kimchi *jjigae*, Korean stew with kimchi and pork.

them. At other *budae-jjigae* establishments, customers can choose from an all-you-can-eat buffet of ingredients and cook their own versions of *budae-jjigae* based on their tastes and ingredient choices.

Many cities in South Korea claim to be the original location for the invention of *budae-jjigae*, but the ultimate origin of the dish is unclear. Uijeongbu is famous for its *budae-jjigae* and boasts a large number of restaurants that specialize in it. The city, which contains the U.S. Army base of Camp Stanley, is north of Seoul, near the Demilitarized Zone (DMZ) with North Korea, making it an important strategic location with a high percentage of American soldiers and easy access to SPAM.

Budae-jjigae has also transcended its usual restaurant setting. Companies such as Ottogi and Samyang now make popular versions of *budae-jjigae*-flavoured ramen noodles available at grocery stores throughout South Korea. The Korean food company Nongshim has created a version of *budae-jjigae* that is

Budae-jjjigae (army stew).

named 'K-Army', or 'Korean Army', ramen. A green army camouflage and a combat hat are on the label's background, while in the foreground, a bubbling pot of *budae-jjigae* is pictured. But the packet of food gives no indication of the impact of American foodways on the Korean dish. The transference of an American-influenced army stew to a Korean Army stew illustrates how fully integrated the food has become in Korean society, linking it directly to Korean identity, and disassociating it from any reference to the Korean War.

Budae-jjigae, like South Korea, is a phoenix rising from the ashes. It shifted from a food for poverty-stricken people, who faced starvation, to being reborn as a communal dish, popular throughout the country. The dish not only symbolizes war and devastation, but represents a triumph over adversity, turning American food into a Korean mainstay through creativity and reinvention.

6
SPAM's Longevity and Enduring Appeal

The end of war did not diminish SPAM's reach into the countries in which it had been used as a means of food support and survival. In all of the countries in which SPAM was doled out by the American government through foreign aid and military intervention, the tinned meat has remained an enduring legacy of conflict and the spread of American foodways across the planet. The reach of the processed food has also permeated everyday life and popular culture to varying degrees in many of these countries. Most prominent are the representations of SPAM in the UK, South Korea, the Philippines and Guam.

Across television, film and theatre of the twentieth and twenty-first centuries, one can catch glimpses of SPAM in both large and small ways. The most iconic depiction of SPAM in post-war television can be seen in a 1970 comedy skit, suitably titled 'Spam', created by the British comedy troupe known as Monty Python – Graham Chapman, John Cleese, Eric Idle, Terry Gilliam, Terry Jones and Michael Palin – for the BBC's *Monty Python's Flying Circus*. The memorable, if improbable, scene is set in a greasy-spoon café in Bromley, London. A group of Vikings is seated around a table on one side of the screen, and they periodically break out into a chorus of 'SPAM, SPAM, SPAM, SPAM, SPAM, lovely SPAM! Wonderful SPAM!' On the other side of the screen is a couple played by Idle as Mr Bun and Chapman dressed in drag as Mrs Bun, who are mulling over the menu, while the waitress (played by Jones), stands by and offers suggestions about what to order. Featured dishes consist of SPAM in all possible combinations, with eggs, sausage or bacon.

The husband in the skit is in favour of SPAM, but his wife does not like it. The sketch pokes fun at SPAM and people's divided opinions about it, suggesting it was cheap and all-too-readily available in less reputable establishments in the UK. The setting of the skit and the characters involved in it suggest that those who consume SPAM in Britain are old-fashioned, out-of-date and most likely working-class individuals who do not possess refined taste in their choice of café or the food that they

Menu on the set of *Monty Python Live (Mostly)*, London, 2014.

Poster for a Broadway production of *Monty Python's Spamalot*, at the Shubert Theatre, New York, 2005.

consume. The scene also portrays the legacy of American SPAM and the long-term impact of U.S. lifestyle and consumption practices on British society.

Taking the joke one step further, Eric Idle, part of the Monty Python comedy group, created the book and lyrics for the play *Spamalot*, which appeared on Broadway in 2005, directed by Mike Nichols. It appeared in London's West End from 2006 to 2009, with subsequent tours in the United States and the UK, and had a Broadway revival in 2023. The title of the play comes from the lyrics to the Camelot song in the 1975 film *Monty Python and the Holy Grail*, in which the Knights of the Round Table sing, 'We eat ham and jam and SPAM a lot.' The film, and subsequent play, parody the legend of King Arthur and the Knights of the Round Table.

Post-war depictions of conflict led to the satirization of SPAM, most notably found in the American television series *M*A*S*H*. The programme, which ran from 1972 to 1983, was a comedy-drama set during the Korean War and depicted the lives of American men and women working in the 4077th U.S. Mobile Army Surgical Hospital in Uijeongbu, South Korea, near the 38th parallel. SPAM figured prominently in the fourteenth episode of the show's third season, 'Private Charles Lamb', which aired on 31 December 1974. In this episode, the characters are invited by a Greek unit to share in their Easter meal, which was to feature lamb as the main course. However, one of the characters, 'Radar', played by Gary Burghoff, objects to the killing of the lamb and instead creates an alternative: SPAM lamb. The episode links with the persistent presence and overabundance of SPAM in the diets of American service personnel during the Korean War.

In 1995, the Jim Henson Company took inspiration from SPAM's long culinary prominence in American culture and created the Muppets character Spa'am for its film *Muppet Treasure*

SPAM lamb in *M*A*S*H**, season 3, episode 14, 'Private Charles Lamb' (1974).

Island, which was released in 1996. In the film, Spa'am is the high priest of wild boars on the island and seeks to install Miss Piggy as the herd's queen. Hormel objected to what they viewed as the misuse of the name, trademark infringement and the possible negative impact on the sale of their product. Hormel sued Jim Henson Productions in the U.S. District Court. However, the judge sided with Henson and rejected Hormel's lawsuit.[1]

The most recent incarnation of SPAM in American popular culture can be viewed in the play *Specially Processed American Me* by Korean American writer Jaime Sunwoo, which premiered in 2022.[2] The play tells the autobiography of the author, using SPAM as the lens through which she depicts the connections between Koreans' everyday life, the Korean American experience and Korean foodways.

The prevalence of SPAM by pop culture icons such as Monty Python demonstrates consumer awareness, and, in some quarters, devotion to the pork product long after the war concluded. Such devotion, or revulsion, to the unusual meat and its unique place in history has inspired creative, even eccentric, responses from the American public, particularly in song and verse. Alfred Matthew Yankovic, better known as 'Weird Al' Yankovic, is an American musician and actor who writes and performs songs that poke comedic fun at pop culture, often through the reworking of famous American tunes. In 1993 Yankovic released *The Food Album*, a compilation of some of the singer's hit songs related to food. Included on the album is the song 'SPAM', which parodies the REM song 'Stand'. In addition, the album includes the songs 'Eat It', based on Michael Jackson's 'Beat It', and 'Addicted to Spuds', based on Robert Palmer's hit 'Addicted to Love'.

SPAM is a versatile substance that people fold into their everyday lives according to their needs, culinary traditions and cultures, enabling diverse experiences with and creative use of the food. Such wide-ranging interactions with and consumption of the processed food have created lasting impressions, both positive and negative, of the food through several generations of people in the United States and abroad. These interactions with SPAM have been memorialized in countless ways, including in poetry. In 1995 John Cho created the SPAM-Ku Archive to enable people to submit haiku about their favourite luncheon meat.[3] Cho, who dubbed himself the SPAM Haiku Archive Master (SHAM), and later the SPAM Haiku Archive Master Emeritus (SHAME) on the website, also set up portals for people to submit other forms of verse about SPAM, such as sonnets and limericks, as well as other miscellaneous writing about the tinned meat.[4] The archive, which collected materials until 2002, contains more than 19,695 haiku. The prose remains online as a symbol of people's enduring fondness for SPAM.

Weeding through this abundant collection of enthusiastic entries, Cho selected the best haiku and compiled them into the book *SPAM-Ku: Tranquil Reflections on Luncheon Loaf.*

Published in 1998, while the archive was still active, the book contains 150 haiku from the collection. The SPAM-Ku Archive also inspired a short film, *SPAM-Ku* (2004), written and directed by Steven K. Tsuchida, which shows the eccentricities around SPAM in popular culture. It depicts a man who has won a SPAM-ku contest. His prize? A lifetime supply of SPAM. All day at work, he dreams about the many ways he will prepare the tinned meat, such as SPAM cupcakes, SPAM nachos and 'SPAM-balia-jumbalia'. He becomes so obsessed with the thought of his prize that when it doesn't turn up at his home, he turns into SPAM itself, sans the tin, fulfilling his dreams. The film takes the character's love of SPAM to the ultimate conclusion, turning consumers into the food that they consume, suggesting the comedy of SPAM, but also serving as a warning that fanaticism over SPAM can go too far.

SPAM's continuing and expanding popularity across the globe is due in no small part to Hormel's extensive, diverse and creative marketing of the product. The company uses many avenues for sales promotion, including social media and online and television advertising to sell its tinned meat. SPAM is present on all major social media sites from Facebook to TikTok, Instagram and Pinterest. Replicating much of the same content across these sites, Hormel posts SPAM recipes, tips, promotions and merchandise for sale. Consumers are encouraged to use SPAM to mark holidays and other important events throughout the year. TikTok is unique in that SPAM fans are encouraged and allowed to upload short videos of themselves cooking and eating SPAM. SPAM even has its own channel on YouTube. The site contains a large amount of both vintage and modern TV commercials advertising the processed food. There is also a collection of cooking videos, so that consumers accessing the site can learn how to cook anything from Korean favourites such as kimbap and *budae-jjigae* to SPAM mac and cheese and SPAM tacos, suggesting that there is no end to the meat's versatility and uses.

Sponsorship comprises an important component of Hormel's strategy to draw customers in and ensure that they remain loyal buyers of the tinned good. In 1996 Hormel joined with the National Association for Stock Car Auto Racing (NASCAR) in the United States and sponsored Lake Speed's car #9, a Ford Thunderbird, as the SPAM car.[5] They repeated their endorsement of a car on the circuit in 1997, this time sponsoring racing driver Mike Wallace's car, #91. NASCAR's popularity provided Hormel with a national platform on which to advertise its product to millions of viewers watching from the stands or through their living room television sets.

Brand mascot characters have also become a useful means by which the SPAM brand is recognized worldwide. Hormel developed a series of characters to mark significant events in the history of SPAM and also to promote the sales growth of the product. Spammy-kun, the original SPAM mascot in the

Sir-Can-A-Lot, SPAM Museum, Austin, Minnesota.

form of the famous blue-labelled tin, rose to popularity in the 1990s, promoting the tinned meat to the world. In 2012 he was joined by Sir-Can-A-Lot to mark the 75th anniversary of SPAM. Sir-Can-A-Lot is a 3.8-centimetre-high (1½ in.) knight, clad in armour and emblazoned with an 'S' for SPAM on his chest and shield.[6] Finally, Musu, a character in the shape of the popular dish SPAM musubi, joined the line-up in 2017 at the Waikiki SPAM Jam in Oahu, Hawaii.

SPAM's popular appeal has been helped by annual festivals, fairs and food contests in the United States. The largest of these is the annual SPAM Jam in Hawaii. The event draws thousands of people to the area to sample traditional and new dishes made with SPAM. The event kicks off with a one-day street party in late April covering several roads in Waikiki, which consists of food vendors selling SPAM in a wide variety of forms, and retailers selling SPAM-inspired goods and other hand-crafted objects. The party is then followed by two weeks in which restaurants in the area feature SPAM dishes on their menus. More than twenty restaurants take part in the festivities, serving up creative SPAM dishes, including SPAM nachos, SPAM gyros, SPAM cupcakes and even cocktails served in SPAM tins. The annual festival not only reinforces the historical legacy of SPAM on the island and the intergenerational sharing of the pork product, but acts as a fundraiser to support local community organizations.

In the 1990s, the home of SPAM, Austin, Minnesota, hosted a festival of its own that paid homage to the food that helped build Hormel, and with it, the town. Held on 4 July, the SPAM Jamboree featured an eating contest, a family walk, a marathon, entertainment and games.[7] Hormel also runs a SPAM food stall at the Great Minnesota Get-Together, which is held annually in the state's largest city, Minneapolis. Here, Hormel sells SPAM burgers, SPAM curds, SPAM breakfast sandwiches and individual tins of SPAM to enthusiasts.

Spamville at the Minnesota State Fair, 2009.

From 1991 to 2019, fairs across the United States played host to the Great American SPAM Championship. From June to November, contestants at 26 county and state fairs submitted their best Hawaiian-themed recipe, using SPAM as the key ingredient. Winners of the local events moved on to the national level competition, which was judged by Hormel representatives at the company's test kitchens. The winner of the grand prize received a trip to Hawaii, where they would attend the SPAM Jam in April. The cooking competition was last held the year before the 2020–23 COVID-19 pandemic. At the time of writing, it is unclear whether this competition will resume in the coming years.[8]

The other Austin – Texas's state capital – used to host a festival known as SPAMARAMA, which was dedicated to the processed meat. The festival ran from 1978 to 2007, and it was again revived in 2019. The event was originally created and organized by David Arnesberger and others as a creative celebration of SPAM on April Fool's Day. The festival hosted a cooking contest, an eating contest and SPAM-themed games such as SPAM toss and tug-of-war, with the losers ending up in a puddle of liquid gel from tins of SPAM.[9] The festival was suspended during the COVID-19 pandemic, but the event was again held on 2 April 2022 and featured the SPAMALYMPICS, which consisted of the SPAM toss, sans tin, the SPAMburger speed-eating contest and a SPAM Call at which the person who provided the most creative, crowd-pleasing way to call out the word 'SPAM' won.[10] The Smithsonian even made a short video documenting the festival, focusing on the cooking competition that formed a key part of the event.[11]

In addition to its advertising and merchandising, Hormel has worked to sustain, renew and reinvigorate people's interest in SPAM by adding new flavours and taste experiences to the product. From 1937 to 1970, original SPAM remained a single product familiar to many in America, Europe and Asia. By 1964 it came in two sizes; the traditional tin, and a smaller, 200-gram (7 oz) tin. But in the 1970s the company began experimenting and adding new flavours under the SPAM banner. In 1971 Hormel introduced SPAM flavoured with cheese known as the 'Hormel Ham and Cheese Loaf' and SPAM with smoke flavour known as SPAM Hickory Smoke Flavored. In 1986 it began manufacturing SPAM with less sodium. The 1990s saw the expansion of the line to include SPAM Lite, with 50 per cent less fat (1995), and SPAM Oven Roasted Turkey (1997). Each decade thereafter saw the continual growth and diversity of SPAM products sold to domestic and international audiences with new and, sometimes, surprising flavours. From 2000 to 2009, Hormel rolled out SPAM Hot & Spicy (2000), SPAM with Real Hormel Bacon (2004) and SPAM Singles (2007). The following decade, the company introduced consumers to SPAM Teriyaki and SPAM Jalapeño (both in 2012). To cater to the popularity of the tinned meat in the Philippines, the company produced SPAM Tocino in 2014, as mentioned in Chapter Four. Hormel's latest versions of the pork product are SPAM Maple Flavored (2023) and SPAM Korean BBQ Flavored (2024).

The company also likes to produce limited-edition versions of SPAM, which mark particular events or seasons. The performance of Monty Python's *Spamalot* on Broadway in 2005 was commemorated by Hormel with the limited-edition SPAM Golden Honey Grail. Following the trend in the food and beverage industry to infuse many products with pumpkin-spice flavour at the start of autumn, Hormel created its limited-edition SPAM Pumpkin Spice in 2019. Finally, in 2022 the company took the classic British Christmas pudding, a cakelike food full of dried fruit and spices and infused with brandy, and turned it into the limited-edition SPAM Figgy Pudding.

Many of these products are not available in every supermarket. Typically, supermarkets in the United States have a few varieties of SPAM on hand, which often include original SPAM, SPAM singles and perhaps SPAM Bacon or SPAM Oven Roasted Turkey. But other varieties of SPAM are more difficult to obtain. They can often be purchased from online shops such as Amazon or, if in the United States, Walmart or Target. The limited editions can vary in price and are often expensive. The other option is to purchase many of the hard-to-find varieties of SPAM from the SPAM Museum in Austin, Minnesota (in-person or online).

Ever malleable to consumer tastes and preferences, SPAM has remained popular in Asia. Companies in China, South Korea and the Philippines have taken the premise of SPAM and built in twenty-first-century tastes by creating plant-based versions to appeal to and accommodate the rise of vegetarian and vegan preferences among consumers. Green Monday, a Hong-Kong-based company, created OmniPork Luncheon meat in 2018. The product aims to mimic pork-based luncheon meat such as SPAM in taste and texture, fulfilling people's love of the original pork-based food while offering a healthier option. Ingredients include soybeans, beets and wheat to produce a product that is much lower in sodium than SPAM. This plant-based version akin to SPAM-like luncheon meat is available throughout Asia and in the United States through shops such as Walmart.

Not to be outdone in the growing vegan food market, the South Korean company Shinsegae Foods, and its U.S. subsidiary, Better Foods, launched the Better Meat line in 2021. The product line, which manufactures products such as meatless meatballs and ham, also produces a vegan luncheon meat, which is similar to SPAM. The product is available in the United States and South Korea.

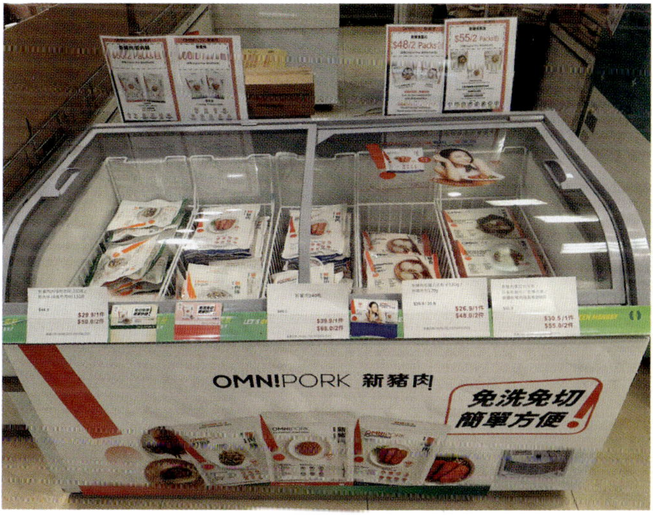

OmniPork Luncheon meat, Hong Kong.

unMEAT, a luncheon meat-style food inspired by SPAM.

The push for healthier, meatless alternatives has also led to product innovation in the Philippines. Filipino-based food company Century Pacific has launched its unMEAT brand, a vegan line of products, which includes SPAM-inspired Luncheon Meat-Style. The ingredients for the meatless food include soy, wheat, seasoning and vinegar. On the unMEAT website, the company claims that the product 'looks, tastes, and cooks just like luncheon meat'.[12] The plant-based food is available in the Philippines, as well as in U.S. shops and online.

Since its inception and use in wartime, SPAM has served as a stabilizing food, helping to feed people in times of food insecurity, economic depression and disasters (natural and man-made). Today, the pork product continues to serve this function in a number of ways. During the COVID-19 pandemic, the tinned good acted as a durable means to obtain a self-stable, long-lasting and inexpensive form of protein, particularly when meat was in short supply in the early days of the virus's outbreak. Having tins of SPAM on the shelves at home reduced the number of trips to the supermarket or grocery store, lowering the possibility of infection. As a result, sales of SPAM skyrocketed not only in the United States but globally, particularly in the Asian market, reaching record highs during this period.[13]

What has become a Korean comfort food also became an important part of the South Korean government's efforts to combat the spread of COVID-19 and support individuals in isolation. At the height of the pandemic, the government provided homebound, isolated individuals with care packages of food, water and medicine. Among the goods provided were the ingredients needed to make *budae-jjigae* at home, which included a knock-off version of SPAM known as Richam Original (리챔).[14]

In 2023 a wildfire swept through the island of Maui, Hawaii, leaving devastation in its wake. Thousands were left without food or shelter. In an effort to provide support and comfort to those in need, Hormel donated 264,000 tins of SPAM to the people of Maui.[15] Because the tinned food was already fully cooked, those who were without cooking facilities were still able to consume it, making it an ideal food for the disaster. SPAM's familiarity and popularity in Hawaii have enabled Hormel, through its provision of food, to provide a little comfort to people in the face of disaster.

Love it or hate it, SPAM fills an important niche in American and international food culture as a ready, self-contained food, which is easily able to aid caloric intake in domestic settings and abroad. Such convenience in transportability, storage and preparation makes it a valuable commodity in disaster situations. SPAM's versatility and sustained popularity the world over will ensure that Hormel continues to see strong sales growth of the tinned good now and into the future.

7

SPAMtown USA

Depending on what is being processed at the Hormel factory, the air in Austin, Minnesota, also known as 'SPAMtown USA', carries the hint of whatever pork products are being processed that day. Some days it smells like cooked ham, others like bacon. The town itself is, in many ways, an ode to the Hormel company. Several restaurants in town offer SPAM dishes on their menus, such as SPAM Benedict at the Barley's Family Restaurant, the SPAM sandwich at B&J Bar and Grill and the SPAM omelette at Kenny's Oak Grill. Many buildings are owned and operated by Hormel and serve as community resources for its staff, their dependents and others living in the town.

Travelling around town, one can see the Hormel Health Center, the Hormel Employment Center, the Hormel Institute (a cancer research lab), various Hormel company offices and the Jay C. Hormel Nature Center. The home of George A. Hormel, which was built in the centre of Austin in 1871 by John Cook, was purchased by Hormel in 1901. In 1982 it was added to the National Register of Historic Places. Today, the Hormel Historic Home offers tours of the house, and various private events are held there throughout the year.

One of the most visible town markers of the pork product is the SPAM Museum, which is located in the middle of Austin. The 1,300-square-metre (14,000 sq. ft) homage to the food that won the war was constructed in 2016 and provides a wealth of information about the tinned good. An earlier, smaller version of the museum was built in 2001 at another site in the city. This second iteration is centrally located and is the main attraction in the town. Thousands of visitors passing through the area each year stop to learn the history of the foodstuff and often reminisce about their own experiences with the food. The building houses the museum, museum gift shop and Hormel offices. The museum is open every day and is free to all visitors, who can wander from exhibit to exhibit on a self-guided tour. They also have the option of taking a tour with a museum docent, known as a 'SPAMbassador'. There are eight galleries in total, which cover wide-ranging topics such as the history of

Hormel Historic Home, 2016.

SPAM Museum, Austin, Minnesota.

the company, its connection to the military and wartime food, how SPAM is produced at the factory and the philanthropic work of the Hormel Foods Corporation. Children can play in a dedicated 88-square-metre (950 sq. ft) SPAM-themed play area. There are touchscreens that enable viewers to take a quiz to see what type of SPAM matches their personality and to browse and email themselves a wide variety of recipes with SPAM from around the world.

Visitors can watch a video of the whole process of SPAM production, from pork shoulder to tin, and they can also time themselves to see how long it takes them to simulate filling a plastic tin of SPAM. The museum is full of loads of eccentric and diverse trinkets, including a SPAM model rocket and other Hormel-related paraphernalia. The museum pays special attention to its global reach with its 'World Market' exhibit. In the displays, guests can search the globe and read information about the countries that sell and consume SPAM, which stretch from North and South America to Europe and the Pacific.

Interior of the SPAM Museum, Austin, Minnesota.

Visitors can also step into designed sets, including a British pub, a Korean temple and a Hawaiian beach bungalow, to see the many SPAM-related products sold in each of these locations. Visitors can also have their pictures taken with the Hormel characters SPAMMY and Sir-Can-A-Lot.

The museum highlights the diverse philanthropic efforts of the company at home and abroad, including its efforts to reverse child malnutrition through its Project SPAMMY in Guatemala. Hormel created 'SPAMMY', a tinned-turkey spread for Guatemalan children, who often lack key vitamins and minerals in their diets. Eating SPAMMY helps support the children's nutritionally balanced diet.

The museum shop is the place to buy all manner of SPAM-themed memorabilia, from shirts and hats, to keychains, magnets and stickers. It is also the only physical location in the world – except perhaps the grocery stores of Austin, Minnesota – where one can buy eleven varieties of SPAM. Food shops around the world sell some varieties of the pork product, but the many types are not all available in any of them.

Diehard fans flock to the museum shop to stock up on the different tins of SPAM and, if buying in bulk, to get a discount. This doesn't extend to the limited-edition varieties of SPAM, which, in some cases, are only available online, such as the 2019 limited-edition pumpkin-spice-flavoured version.

In a town that covers nearly 31 square kilometres (12 sq. mi.) and has a population of 26,000 people, Hormel is the largest employer in the area, providing jobs for more than 1,800 workers.[1] Although the factory has moved from its original site to

World Market exhibit at the SPAM Museum designed to look like a traditional British pub, with eclectic window display.

expand its production capacity, it is still possible to visit one of the original buildings at the Mower County Pioneer and Historical Society.

Today the Hormel factory, which sits on the eastern side of town, is a constant hive of activity, with deliveries coming in and shipments going out at all hours of the day. The Hormel site constitutes a series of several large production buildings and corporate offices. The total size of the factory is 120,770 square metres (1.3 million sq. ft), which churns out 450 million kilograms (1 billion lb) of Hormel pork products every year.[2] In tribute to its most famous and one of its bestselling foodstuffs, Hormel has commissioned a 1.5-metre-tall (5 ft) SPAM statue, which sits on the factory grounds.

Despite its dominance in the town, the company and its workers have not always coexisted in harmony. In 1985 the company, citing an economic downturn, demanded that workers settle for a 23 per cent cut in wages to weather the financial

Varieties of SPAM on the shelves of a shop in Austin, Minnesota.

SPAM can sculpture outside the Hormel administrative building in Austin, Minnesota.

uncertainty. However, workers did not support such a cut, and in August 1985, 1,500 employees walked off the job and went on strike. The labour strike turned into a ten-month standoff between workers and the company, which at certain points turned unruly and required the National Guard to help contain the situation. Finally, the strike ended – unsuccessfully for members of the union – in June 1986. The high-profile and protracted nature of the dispute inspired the Academy Award-winning documentary *American Dream* (1990), directed by Barbara Kopple, Cathy Caplan, Thomas Haneke and Lawrence Silk, which tells the story of the strike.

During the COVID-19 pandemic, many food manufacturers were forced to shut down in the early days of the outbreak, causing a dearth of meat and other products in shops across the United States. The pork industry was deemed an 'essential' business by the federal government, and the Hormel plant stayed open throughout the lockdown that closed so many other business operations. However, the close proximity of the workers in the plant led to high rates of illness, particularly during the early months of the virus's spread. In June 2020, the *Austin Daily Herald* ran an article that detailed how more than two hundred workers tested positive for the virus.[3] The continuation of operations at Hormel enabled the pork products to continue flowing to consumers and allowed the company to meet the spike in demand and fulfil the supply gap caused by the closure of other food plants. The public health crisis sent the sale of SPAM and other Hormel products soaring. According to Hormel's website, the company's sale of SPAM in the second quarter of 2020 reached double-digit growth.[4]

Continuing its commitment to the Austin community, Hormel also supported the consumption needs of seniors as well as children aged one to eighteen during the crisis by providing them with free meals.[5] As it was originally designed to do, SPAM once again offered a measure of food security in uncertain times.

Recipes

United States and Europe

SPAM and Eggs

One of the classic ways to eat SPAM is as part of a hearty breakfast with eggs. Variations of the classic SPAM and eggs recipes abound. The eggs can be fried or scrambled. The eggs can be eaten plain, or they can be augmented with cheese or other complementary foods.

1 standard (340 g/12 oz) tin SPAM (Classic or other variety)
olive oil or butter, for frying
2 eggs per person
2 slices bread per person

Remove SPAM from the tin and cut into slices of desired thickness. In a large skillet, add oil or butter, enough to coat the bottom of the pan. Over medium heat, brown both sides of the SPAM slices. Remove the slices and place on a plate. Add additional oil or butter to coat the pan. Then crack eggs into the pan. Cook eggs to desired consistency. While eggs are cooking, toast slices of bread in a toaster. Remove the eggs from the pan and place them on the plate with the SPAM. Remove toast from the toaster, butter and place on the plate next to the SPAM and eggs. Serve warm.
Serves 2–3

SPAM Sandwich

A SPAM sandwich is a quick and easy meal to make, particularly if time is short. This is one of the main ways that SPAM has been eaten the world over, and it was a particularly popular way to consume the tinned good in the United States before and during the Second World War. This dish is good for a packed lunch or a quick supper.

1 standard tin SPAM (choose the variety of SPAM that you prefer)
2 pieces of bread per slice of SPAM
cheese (optional)
lettuce and/or tomato (optional)
condiments of choice (optional)

Remove SPAM from the tin and cut into slices of medium thickness, cutting along the long side. Spread condiment of choice on two slices of bread. Lay a slice of SPAM on one slice over the condiment spread, and then cover with the other slice of bread, condiment-spread-side facing in. The sandwich can be served at room temperature or warm.

If adding cheese, add a slice to the inside of the SPAM sandwich, and then warm the sandwich in the microwave or in a panini press or toastie maker. Alternatively, coat a pan with a little oil, and brown both sides of the sandwich. (Add toppings, such as lettuce and tomato on top of the cheese, if desired.)

Add a condiment of choice – this is entirely down to your preference. Popular choices include mustard, ketchup, mayonnaise, butter, cheese, horseradish and sriracha, among others. Other possible sandwich toppings include pickle, relish and so forth. Serve warm.

SPAM Bake

Adapted from advertisement for SPAM, 'SPAM: The Meat of Many Uses', *Ladies' Home Journal*, LVI/12 (December 1939), p. 68

This dish originated during the Great Depression, when SPAM was a new product on the American market. Adapting the traditional recipe for baked ham, Americans used the cheaper pork, SPAM, to create the same dish.

1 standard tin Classic SPAM
whole cloves
70 g (⅓ cup) light brown sugar
2 tsp water

Preheat the oven to 200 °C (400°F). Remove SPAM from the tin and cut shallow cross hatches across the entire surface of the pork. Stud the outside of the SPAM with cloves along the slits cut into the meat, and place in a baking pan. Mix the brown sugar and water. Coat the outside of the SPAM with the liquid mixture, and put in the oven. Cook the meat for 30 minutes. Remove from the oven and serve warm.
Serves 3–4

SPAM and Spaghetti

Ladies' Home Journal, LIX/5 (May 1942), p. 104

The recipe is adapted from a Hormel advertisement in *Ladies' Home Journal* in 1942, the year that food rationing started in the United States. The advert advises women on ways to feed their husbands. It suggests making spaghetti or macaroni and cheese to pair with SPAM.

spaghetti – amount as desired, depending on the number of people to feed
water
vegetable oil
1 standard tin SPAM
lemon, to dress (optional)
chopped spring onions, to garnish (optional)
olive oil, to dress (optional)

Fill a pasta pot about three-quarters full with water and set to boil. Once boiling, add spaghetti to cook. This will take approximately

20 minutes. While the spaghetti is cooking, open a tin of SPAM, and cut into cubes. Add a small amount of oil to a frying or sauté pan to coat. Bring the temperature of the pan up to medium heat and add the SPAM. Brown on both sides. This will take approximately 5–7 minutes. When completed, remove from the pan and set on a plate. When spaghetti is ready, drain and serve on a plate with the cubes of SPAM. If adding lemon, squeeze the juice and pour a little oil over the pasta; garnish with spring onion (optional). Serve warm.

SPAM and Beans

Adapted from advertisement for SPAM in *Ladies' Home Journal*, LIX/2 (February 1942), p. 78

This is a classic dish that combines two American staples, SPAM and beans. It is a hearty dish adapted from a 1942 advert.

1 340-gram (12 oz) tin beans (such as haricot (navy) beans)
1 standard tin SPAM
light brown sugar, for sprinkling

Preheat the oven to 190°C (375°F). Open a tin of beans and place at the bottom of a baking pan. Open a tin of SPAM, and cut into slices of medium thickness. Lay the slices over the top of the beans in the baking pan. Sprinkle with brown sugar, and place in the oven. Cook until the dish is bubbling and the brown sugar has dissolved. Serve warm.

SPAM 'Birds'

Adapted from advertisement for SPAM in *Ladies' Home Journal*, LXII/4 (April 1945), p. 146.

The recipe is reminiscent of a Thanksgiving or Christmas meal, with stuffing playing a starring role. The 1945 advert was produced at the end of the Second World War.

1 standard tin SPAM
400 g (2 cups) stuffing (for this you can make your own recipe, or buy a stuffing mix and follow directions)

Preheat the oven to 190°C (375°F). Open a tin of SPAM and cut medium-sized slices from the long side. Make the stuffing (recipe or box mix). Lay slices of SPAM on a baking sheet. Place a small amount of stuffing in the middle of the slice, and roll up the sides, making a cylinder with the stuffing inside. Taking a toothpick, stitch the sides together at either side of the cylinder. Bake in the oven until brown. Serve warm.

Serves 3–4

SPAM Fritters

Adapted from Marguerite Patten, *SPAM: The Cookbook* (London, 2001), p. 59

This is a classic British dish that was invented in the Second World War. It can still be found in the frozen section of many grocery stores, as well as fish and chip shops throughout the UK.

1 standard tin SPAM
1 egg
125 g (1 cup) plain (all-purpose) flour
120 ml (½ cup) milk
pinch of salt
olive oil for frying

Remove SPAM from the tin and cut into thick slices. Crack egg, and whisk together with milk and flour, while adding a pinch of salt to form a batter. Place oil in a frying pan and heat up. Meanwhile, dredge each SPAM slice in the batter. Place the battered slices in the frying pan and brown on both sides. Place a paper towel on a plate, and set fritters on the plate to get rid of excessive oil. Consume warm.

Serves 3–4

SPAM and Tripe

Adapted from 'For the Housewife – Lady Edith's Hints',
Belfast News-letter (14 February 1942), p. 4

Offal, such as tripe, kidneys, brain and heart, became an important and much sought-after food during the Second World War. Before the war, offal was an unpopular foodstuff, though women did use it in their cookery. Many housewives turned to it in wartime because it was off-ration, and cooking it enabled them to stretch resources and conserve valuable meat coupons. However, the high demand for offal led to shortages of the meat.

230 g (½ lb) tripe
2 stalks of celery
1 medium cooking onion
1 medium carrot
250–475 ml (1–2 cups) milk for tripe
30 g (¼ cup) plain (all-purpose) flour
4 tbsp butter or margarine
2 tbsp chopped parsley
salt and pepper to taste
1 standard tin SPAM
2 large baking potatoes
250 ml (1 cup) milk (for the mashed potatoes)

Rinse and chop the tripe into medium-sized cubes. Chop up onion, carrot and celery. Combine these ingredients in a pan and cover with milk. Boil on medium-low heat until the tripe is tender, which will take a couple of hours. Make a roux by first melting 1 tbsp of butter, and then adding 1 tbsp of flour. Mix until it becomes a thick paste. Add a cup of the liquid that remains from cooking the tripe to the roux, and stir continually until the liquid thickens into a sauce with a gravy consistency. Strain the contents from the tripe pan, and place in a mixing bowl. Add SPAM and parsley to the bowl. Season with salt and pepper to taste. Pour in the sauce and mix. Fill a new medium-sized saucepan up halfway with water and bring to a boil. In the meantime, cut potatoes into medium-sized pieces. Add

potato pieces to the water and boil until tender. Remove from heat and strain. In a mixing bowl, mash the potatoes, add warm 120 ml (½ cup) of milk as needed and 3 tbsp of butter. Season with salt and pepper. In a pie dish, spoon in the tripe, SPAM and vegetable mixture. Then cover with the mashed potatoes. Bake until the dish is bubbling and the potato top has turned a golden brown.
Serves 3–4

Escalope Amigoni

Adapted from 'Every Woman's Recipes', *The Sketch* (8 April 1942), p. 5.

This dish is originally an Italian recipe, which is often made with breaded chicken. This is a wartime version of the dish, which includes SPAM as the main source of protein.

3 large carrots
1 medium-sized cooking onion
2 stalks of celery
olive oil, for frying
1 standard tin SPAM
breadcrumbs (use enough to coat the pieces of SPAM evenly)
1 egg
milk (use enough to dip SPAM into)

Chop the carrots, celery and onion. Add olive oil to coat the bottom of a frying pan, and sauté the vegetables until soft and slightly brown. Cut SPAM into slices of medium thickness on the long side. Crack egg onto a plate, add a small amount of milk and mix. Pour breadcrumbs onto another plate. Dredge the slices of SPAM first in the egg mixture, and then in the breadcrumbs. Pour olive oil into a frying pan and add the slices of battered SPAM. Brown on both sides. Plate the vegetables and then add a slice of fried SPAM. Serve warm.
Serves 3–4

SPAM Macaroni and Cheese

Macaroni and cheese is a classic American dish, which can be made in a variety of ways and with a variety of ingredients.

400 g (4 cups) macaroni
1 standard tin SPAM
30 g (¼ cup) plain (all-purpose) flour
55 g (4 tbsp) butter
600 ml (2½ cups) milk
450 g (1 lb) grated cheese (cheddar is traditional, but gouda, mozzarella or fontina are possible options)
salt and pepper, to taste
breadcrumbs (enough to cover the noodle mixture in the pan)

Boil the macaroni in hot water, and drain once cooked. Open tin of SPAM and cut into small cubes. In a saucepan, melt the butter, and then add flour. Stir until a thick paste is formed. Slowly add milk and stir until thickened. Add the cheese and stir until melted. Season with salt and pepper to taste. In a mixing bowl, combine the pasta, SPAM and creamy sauce. Pour the contents of the mixing bowl into a baking pan. Sprinkle the breadcrumbs over the mixture until the dish is covered. Bake until the dish is bubbling and the breadcrumbs are golden brown. Serve warm.
Serves 3–4

SPAM Musubi (Hawaii)

Adapted from Jean Watanabe Hee, *Little Hawaiian Cookbook* (Honolulu, 2006), p. 14

This is a popular dish eaten throughout the Hawaiian Islands, as well as throughout Asia. It is similar in structure to Korean kimbap, as well as a variation on a form of Japanese sushi.

1 standard tin SPAM
4 sheets large, dried, pressed seaweed

500 g (2½ cups) cooked rice
soy sauce or roasted sesame oil, for dipping (optional)

Cut SPAM into medium-thick strips lengthwise. At one end of the long side of a sheet of seaweed, place a row of rice. On top of the rice, place a layer of SPAM strips. Then roll the rice and SPAM inside the seaweed. Repeat process with remaining ingredients. Once all of the seaweed is rolled, cut perpendicularly across each roll to make circular pieces. Place on a plate and serve at room temperature. Provide a dish of soy sauce and/or sesame oil in a small-sized dish for dipping discs of SPAM musubi.
Serves 3–4

SPAM Salad

The recipe is an adaptation of a traditional Cobb salad that uses SPAM, rather than ham.

4 hard-boiled eggs
1 tin of SPAM
head of lettuce
½ cup olive oil
¼ cup lemon juice, freshly squeezed
1½ tbsp English mustard
salt and pepper
1 medium-sized cucumber
250 g (1 cup) cherry tomatoes or similar small-sized tomatoes
225 g (8 oz) crumbled feta or blue cheese

Boil the eggs. Remove from the pan, and let cool in cold water. Open the tin of spam and cut into medium-sized slices. Wash and tear the head of lettuce into pieces. Mix two parts olive oil to one part lemon juice and one part mustard. Add a pinch of salt and pepper to the dressing. Once eggs are cool, remove shells and cut into slices. Cut cucumber into slices. Cut tomatoes in half. Combine eggs, cucumbers, tomatoes, SPAM mixture, and cheese, in a bowl, add dressing, mix and serve cold over lettuce pieces.

SPAM Charcuterie Board

In recent years, offering a charcuterie board, a tradition of French and Italian (as *antipasto*) cuisine, as a starter at parties and in restaurants has become a popular practice in the United States and in the UK too. This dish typically includes two to three types of cured meat such as prosciutto, mortadella and salami. To the meat offerings, add cubes of any type of SPAM. If a slightly spicier version of SPAM is wanted, use SPAM Jalapeño. Two to three cheeses are offered alongside these meats, such as brie, camembert and cheddar. Crackers or bread are also used to accompany the cheese. Two to three types of olives are included such as Kalamata, Castelvetrano and Spanish olives. Dried fruits and nuts, such as apricots and dried cherries, cashews, almonds and peanuts are common accompaniments.

Guam

Kelaguen with SPAM

Adapted from recipe found in Dorothy Horn, *Great Classic SPAM Recipes of the World: From Dorothy's Kitchen* (Hong Kong, 1994), p. 72

This Guamanian dish was traditionally made with a protein such as chicken or seafood. But since the arrival of SPAM, it is also now made with the tinned pork as the main protein of the dish. The recipe mixes the heat from chillies with the acidity of lemons and sweetness of coconut; chillies, lemons and coconut are all native ingredients to the island. SPAM is the foreign agent introduced as a result of the Second World War.

1 standard tin SPAM
60 ml (¼ cup) lemon juice (add more if you like
a stronger lemon flavour)
2 peppers – hot or bell pepper – diced (depending on spice level)
70 g (¾ cup) coconut – fresh or dried grated (unsweetened)
4 tbsp chopped spring onions
salt to taste

Cut SPAM into small chunks. Dice peppers. Grate coconut (if not using ready-grated coconut). Combine all ingredients together. Serve cold.
Serves 3–4

Philippines

Spamsilog

This dish is commonly eaten as a breakfast item. The name for this dish comes from a combination of words in the Tagalog language. *Silog* is a type of traditional Filipino breakfast that combines some sort of meat such as beef, chicken or ham and fried rice (*sinangag*) and fried eggs (*itlog*). The influx of SPAM into Filipino foodways as a result of the American military influence during the Second World War led to the creation of Spamsilog. It remains a popular variation of the traditional *silog* to this day.

1 tin SPAM (Classic SPAM is the usual variety that is used,
but any type of SPAM will work well in this recipe)
olive oil or butter, for frying (depending on preference)
2 or 3 cloves garlic (this amount can be adjusted for taste;
more can be added if you prefer)
175 g (1 cup) cooked rice – white rice is the classic rice used,
but other types of rice can be used, such as brown rice
1–2 eggs

Cut the SPAM into thick or medium slices, depending on preference. Add enough oil or butter in a skillet to coat the pan and heat; add slices of SPAM, and brown on both sides. Remove the SPAM from the pan. Cut garlic into thin pieces. Add a little more oil or butter to the skillet and sauté the pieces of garlic for 1–2 minutes. Then add the cooked rice to the garlic and cook on medium-low heat for 5–7 minutes. Remove garlic rice from the pan and set aside. Add a little more oil or butter, and cook eggs in pan. Eggs can be cooked to your own preferences. Traditionally, eggs are fried. Serve warm.

Serves 3–4

Okinawa, Japan

Chanpurū

Adapted from recipe for 'Tofu Chanpurū', Allrecipes, www.allrecipes.com

One of the classic dishes of Okinawa is a stir-fry, or *chanpurū*, which means a 'mixed dish', which combines a wide variety of ingredients, such as meat or fish, and tofu, vegetables and eggs. The influx of SPAM as a result of wartime occupation resulted in the inclusion of SPAM into some versions of the dish.

340 g (12 oz) extra-firm tofu
1 tbsp fresh ginger, minced
150 g (½ cup) miso paste
2 tbsp white sugar
120 ml (½ cup) sake
60 ml (¼ cup) soy sauce
vegetable oil, for frying
4 eggs
4 cloves garlic (add more cloves as you prefer)
1 standard tin SPAM (Classic variety)

1 stalk of spring onion, chopped (optional as a garnish)
2 carrots, grated
1 large cooking onion
8 button mushrooms
1 medium head of green cabbage

Drain tofu and cut into 1.25-centimetre (½ in.) squares. In a bowl, mix minced fresh ginger, miso paste, white sugar, sake and soy sauce. Coat a skillet with vegetable oil and brown the tofu. Remove tofu from the pan and set on a plate. Whisk eggs. Coat the skillet again with vegetable oil, pour in eggs, and scramble. When eggs are cooked, set aside. Cut garlic into small pieces and sauté in the skillet with a little oil. Remove garlic from the pan. Cut SPAM into medium-sized strips, add a little more vegetable oil, brown meat on both sides, and remove from the pan. Chop onion, carrot, cabbage and mushrooms. Add more vegetable oil, and sauté these vegetables for 10–12 minutes until the onions turn translucent and the carrots, cabbage and mushrooms are thoroughly cooked. Add tofu, eggs, SPAM and soy sauce mixture to the vegetables in the skillet and stir fry for 1–2 minutes. Sprinkle chopped spring onion over the dish. Serve warm.
Serves 3–4

Korea

Budae-Jjigae

Adapted from 'Budae Jjigae (Army Stew)',
My Korean Kitchen, https://mykoreankitchen.com

This stew was created in war-torn South Korea with the scarce resources available at the time, so that it could be shared between family or friends. This recipe reflects the melding of the Korean tradition of hot pot with many American ingredients that were available at the time in the country. Today *budae-jjigae* is a popular comfort food for many young South Koreans. This recipe contains many of the basic ingredients found in a variety of *budae-jjigaes*, but the contents of the dish can vary widely.

Dry ingredients:
200 g (7 oz) SPAM
140 g (5 oz) of sausage
250 g (9 oz) tofu
30 g (1 oz) spring onion
2 slices American cheese
200 g (7 oz) baked beans
75 g (½ cup) kimchi
200 g (7 oz) shiitake mushrooms
115 g (4 oz) plain ramen noodle
60 g (2 oz) Korean rice cakes

Wet ingredients:
1 tbsp soy sauce
½ tbsp sugar
1 tbsp garlic
2 tbsp rice wine
950 ml (4 cups) beef or chicken stock
½ tbsp gochujang
2 tbsp gochugaru

Cut the SPAM, tofu and sausage into slices. Cut up the spring onions into small pieces. In a deep pot, combine all the dry ingredients except for the ramen noodles and rice cakes. In a separate bowl, combine the wet ingredients. Then pour liquid into a deep pot and bring the contents to a boil. Cover the pot and cook for approximately 8–10 minutes. Then add the ramen noodles and rice cakes to the pot, and let the contents cook for a few extra minutes until the ramen and rice cakes are soft and cooked. Serve warm.

Kimchi *bokkeumbap*

Recipe adapted from a Kimchi fried rice (*kimchi bokkeumbap*) recipe by Maangchi, also known as Emily Kim, a South Korean cook and YouTuber

This is a Korean dish that is often made without a protein. Here, SPAM is added to infuse a pork flavour into the dish.

1 standard tin SPAM
1 tsp vegetable or olive oil
150 g (1 cup) kimchi (older kimchi that has fermented longer is best; new kimchi won't have the sour flavour that is desired for this recipe)
600 g (3 cups) cooked rice (white rice is popular with this dish, but brown rice or other types of rice can be used)
60 ml (¼ cup) kimchi juice from kimchi container (use more if needed, particularly if you like it spicier)
2 tbsp gochujang (more can be added while cooking or eating it, if you like it spicier)
60 ml (¼ cup) water
1 tbsp roasted sesame seeds
3 tsp toasted sesame oil

Optional ingredients for garnish:
1 sheet of roasted, dried seaweed, also known as 'gim', shredded
2–3 fried eggs
1 spring onion, chopped

Cut the SPAM into cubes, place in a skillet, and sauté in vegetable or olive oil for two minutes. Add the kimchi and continue to sauté for another minute. Add the cooked rice, kimchi juice, gochujang and water and cook on medium heat for 7–10 minutes. Turn off the heat and add the sesame oil, sesame seeds and any of the optional ingredients as you wish (shredded seaweed, fried eggs and spring onion). Serve warm.
Serves 3–4

Kimchi *Jjigae*

Adapted from Naomi Imatome-Yun, *Seoul Food: Korean Cookbook* (Berkeley, CA, 2015), p. 113

This dish is a classic Korean hot pot that traditionally includes pork or beef. SPAM is added as an alternative meat.

2 spring onions
2 cloves garlic
½ medium, sweet onion
300 g (2 cups) kimchi
1 standard tin SPAM, thinly sliced
1 tbsp sesame oil
1 tbsp gochugaru
1 tbsp gochujang
700 ml (3 cups) water
1 tbsp soy sauce
340 g (12 oz) firm tofu

Chop the spring onions, garlic and onion. Sauté the SPAM in sesame oil for a couple of minutes in a soup pot. Add the kimchi and continue to sauté. Add the remaining ingredients, apart from the tofu and spring onions, and bring to a boil. Reduce the heat and let simmer for approximately 15 minutes. Add the tofu and continue simmering for another 15 minutes. Serve hot with spring onions on top.

References

Foreword

1 For examples, see R. Broad and S. Fleming, eds, *Nella Last's War: The Second World War Diaries of 'Housewife, 49'* (London, 2006); S. Garfield, ed., *Private Battles: How the War Almost Defeated Us* (London, 2006); P. Holden, ed., *Worthington at War: The Diary of C. F. Harriss* (Chichester, 2010); see the British Newspaper Archive, www.britishnewspaperarchive.co.uk.

Introduction

1 'What is SPAM® Brand?', SPAM Brand, www.spam.com, accessed 1 June 2024.
2 Ibid.
3 Ibid.

1 SPAM to the Rescue: The Business and Politics of Processed Food

1 'Immigration and Relocation in U.S. History: German: A New Surge of Growth', Library of Congress, www.loc.gov, accessed 3 August 2024.

2 Max Kade Institute for German-American Studies, 'How German Is American? Settling in America', University of Wisconsin Madison, https://mki.wisc.edu, accessed 5 August 2024.
3 'Buffalo's Neighborhoods: Exploring Our Migrant and Immigrant Heritage: Buffalo's East Side Deutschtum', New York Heritage Digital Collections, https://nyheritage.org, accessed 3 August 2024.
4 Richard Dougherty, *In Quest of Quality: Hormel's First 75 Years* (St Paul, MN, 1966), pp. 4, 6–8, 9.
5 Doniver Adolph Lund, *The Hormel Legacy: 100 Years of Quality* (Austin, MN, 1991), pp. 8–9, 11–12.
6 Dougherty, *In Quest of Quality*, p. 63.
7 Ibid., p. 39.
8 Ibid., p. 75.
9 Lund, *The Hormel Legacy*, p. 40.
10 Dougherty, *In Quest of Quality*, pp. 117–18.
11 'Great Depression Facts', Franklin D. Roosevelt Presidential Library and Museum, www.fdrlibrary.org, accessed 3 August 2024.
12 Ibid.
13 Dougherty, *In Quest of Quality*, p. 159; Lund, *The Hormel Legacy*, p. 69.
14 'Company News of the Month', *The Squeal: Hormel News-Magazine* (1 July 1937), p. 3.
15 Dougherty, *In Quest of Quality*, pp. 159–61.
16 Carolyn Wyman, *SPAM: A Biography* (New York, 1999), pp. 59–60.
17 Dougherty, *In Quest of Quality*, p. 163.

2 SPAM and the March to War

1 Franklin Delano Roosevelt, 'Fireside Chat', 29 December 1940, p. 8, Franklin D. Roosevelt Presidential Library and Museum, www.fdrlibrary.org, accessed 3 August 2024.

2 Lend-Lease Bill (10 January 1941), U.S. House of Representatives, HR 77A-D13, Record Group 233, National Archives.
3 For a detailed discussion on Congressional voting of Lend-Lease Act, see Warren F. Kimball, *The Most Unsordid Act: Lend-Lease, 1939–1941* (Baltimore, MD, 1969), pp. 195–229.
4 Horace Taylor, *How Shall Lend-Lease Accounts Be Settled?* (Washington, DC, 1945), p. 22.
5 Ibid., p. 18.
6 Ibid., p. 22.
7 Richard Dougherty, *In Quest of Quality: Hormel's First 75 Years* (St Paul, MN, 1966), p. 176.
8 Ibid., p. 181.
9 Taylor, *How Shall Lend-Lease Accounts Be Settled?*, p. 23.
10 Dougherty, *In Quest of Quality*, p. 179; See also 'Homelites – Cvinaya Tushonka', *The Squeal: Hormel News-Magazine* (April 1943), pp. 4–5.
11 Amy Bentley, *Eating for Victory: Food Rationing and the Politics of Domesticity* (Champaign, IL, 1998), p. 115.
12 Ibid., p. 102.
13 Dougherty, *In Quest of Quality*, p. 184.
14 'The Flavor-Sealed Division: Uncle Sam and the Flavor-Sealed Division', *The Squeal*: *Hormel News-Magazine* (March 1942), p. 12.
15 For more discussion of the impact of tin rationing on its production output, see Dougherty, *In Quest of Quality*, pp. 182–3; see also 'The Flavor-Sealed Division', *The Squeal*, p. 12.
16 Jonathan E. Vespa, 'Those Who Served: America's Veterans from the Second World War to the War on Terror: American Community Survey Report', United States Census Bureau, www.census.gov, accessed 3 August 2024.
17 George A. Hormel, *The Open Road: Autobiography of George A. Hormel* (Austin, MN, 2019), p. 328.
18 'Editorial', *The Squeal*: *Hormel News-Magazine* (March 1943), p. 6.
19 Dougherty, *In Quest of Quality*, p. 181.

20 Ibid., p. 191.

21 'From the Field', *The Squeal: Hormel News-Magazine* (April 1943), pp. 12–13; 'From the Field', *Squeal: Hormel News-Magazine* (May 1943), pp. 12–13; 'From the Field', *Squeal: Hormel News-Magazine* (June 1943), pp. 12–15.

3 SPAM on the British Home Front

1 For details about the British black market in the Second World War, see Mark Roodhouse, *Black Market Britain, 1939–1955* (Oxford, 2013).

2 Horace Taylor, *How Shall Lend-Lease Accounts Be Settled?* (Washington, DC, 1945), p. 23.

3 Ibid., p. 22.

4 Kate McMullin, 'Where Did SPAM Come From?', *Liverpool Echo*, www.liverpoolecho.co.uk, 13 February 2017, accessed 3 August 2024.

5 'The Packing Division', *The Squeal: The Hormel News-Magazine* (January 1942), p. 9; see also photo of Lend-Lease goods made by Hormel, *The Squeal: The Hormel News-Magazine* (February 1942), p. 3.

6 'Winning on Points', *Rochdale Observer* (3 January 1942), p. 4; see also 'Points about Points', *Uxbridge and W. Dayton Gazette* (2 January 1942), p. 6.

7 J. Woulfe, 'Warship Week', *Middlesex Chronicle* (31 January 1942), p. 2. Prem is a canned meat similar to SPAM, and was created in 1939 in the United States.

8 W. M. Robertson, 'Public Notices', *Northern Daily Mail* (20 March 1942), p. 2.

9 'For the Housewife – Lady Edith's Hints', *Belfast News-Letter* (14 February 1942), p. 4.

10 See Kelly A. Spring, '"Today We Have All Got to Be Fighting Fit": The Interconnectivity of Gender Roles in British Food Rationing Propaganda during the Second World War', *Gender and History*, XXXII/2 (July 2020), pp. 320–40.

11 'At the Plant: Letter', *The Squeal: Hormel News-Magazine* (June 1942), p. 7.
12 'The Sandwich', *Liverpool Echo* (25 June 1943), p. 4.
13 P. J. Atkins, 'Communal Feeding in War Time: British Restaurants, 1940–1947', in *Food and War in Twentieth Century Europe*, ed. Ina Zweiniger-Bargielowska, Rachel Duffett and Alain Drouard (London, 2011), pp. 139–54.
14 'Hoteliers Look Forward', *West Sussex Gazette* (3 February 1944), p. 4.
15 Bertha Jordan, 'Echo and Gossip of the Day: A Matter of Taste', *Liverpool Echo* (8 January 1943), p. 4.
16 See Ellen Ross, *Love and Toil: Motherhood in Outcast London, 1870–1918* (Oxford, 1993), pp. 32–6.
17 For a discussion of male manual workers' dissatisfaction with the basic adult meat ration, see Ina Zweiniger-Bargielowska, *Austerity in Britain: Rationing, Controls, and Consumption, 1939–1955* (Oxford, 2000), pp. 74–6.
18 'Wearside Echo: Shipyard "Grouses"', *Sunderland Daily Echo and Shipping Gazette* (29 October 1943), p. 2.
19 'By the Way: The New Priority', *Shields Daily News* (23 February 1943), p. 7.
20 Harold S. Stewart, 'Adventure in Eating', *Daily Record* (3 June 1944), p. 2.
21 For more details about SPAM Appreciation Week, see Helen McGurk, 'Get Ready for SPAM Appreciation Week!', *Belfast News Letter* (27 February 2023); 'SPAM® Can Tour to Hit the UK', *Grocery Trader*, https://grocerytrader.co.uk, 3 April 2016.

4 SPAM in the Pacific

1 Robert F. Rogers, *Destiny's Landfall: A History of Guam* (Honolulu, HI, 1995), p. 200.
2 Ibid., pp. 197–8, 200.

3 Ibid., p. 202; see also Dominica Tolentino, 'CHamoru's Love of Spam', *Guampedia*, www.guampedia.com, accessed 3 August 2024.

4 Rogers, *Destiny's Landfall*, pp. 200, 202.

5 Kyla P. Mora, 'The Wartime Alliance of Guam and Spam, Generations Later', *Pacific Daily News*, www.guampdn.com, 22 July 2017.

6 See 'Philippines Country Profile', www.foodexport.org, accessed 14 August 2024.

7 Adam Givens, 'Guardians on the Periphery: The U.S. Army in Hawaii', National WWII Museum, New Orleans, www.nationalww2museum.org, 12 November 2021.

8 See Mire Koikari, 'Love! Spam: Food, Military and Empire in Post-Second World War Okinawa', in *Devouring Japan: Global Perspectives on Japanese Culinary Identity*, ed. Nancy K. Stalker (Oxford, 2018), pp. 171–86.

9 'What is SPAM® Brand?', SPAM Brand, www.spam.com, accessed 1 June 2024.

10 Mora, 'The Wartime Alliance of Guam and Spam'.

11 Takahiro Takiguchi, 'Taste of Okinawa: SPAM Big Part of Island's Culture', *Stripes Okinawa*, https://okinawa.stripes.com, 5 October 2023.

12 Koikari, 'Love!', p. 176.

13 'Japan', Hormel Foods, www.hormelfoods.com, accessed 3 August 2024; see also Okinawa Hormel Foods International, https://okinawahormel.co.jp, accessed 3 August 2024.

14 Stephanie Marcus, 'Burger King Introduces SPAM Burgers for the Women of Japan', *Huffington Post*, www.huffpost.com, 15 August 2011.

15 See Jef®, https://jefokinawa.co.jp, accessed 6 October 2024.

16 'What is SPAM Brand?'

17 Kaile Hunt, 'McDonald's Food that You Can Only Get In Hawaii', KHON2, www.khon2.com, 30 June 2022.

18 James Song, 'Burger King Fighting SPAM War with McDonalds in Hawaii', *Seattle Times*, www.seattletimes.com, 13 June 2007.

19 Cassie Ordonio, 'It's No Secret Hawai-i Loves SPAM. But Health Experts Fear Its Long-Term Risks', Hawai'i Public Radio, www.hawaiipublicradio.org, 22 May 2023; see Laura Williamson, 'Native Hawaiian and Pacific Islander Adults Have Second-Highest Cardiovascular Death Rate in the U.S.', *American Heart Association*, www.heart.org, 8 November 2023.

5 SPAM and the Korean War

1 CNN Editorial Research, 'Korean War Fast Facts', CNN, https://edition.cnn.com, 21 July 2023.
2 Andrew C. Nahm and James Hoare, *Historical Dictionary of the Republic of Korea*, 2nd edn (Lanham, MD, 2004), p. 111.
3 National Park Service, 'Korean War Overview', Korean War Veterans Memorial, www.nps.gov, accessed 3 August 2024.
4 Ibid.; David Vergun, 'America Marks 70th Anniversary of End of Korean War', U.S. Army, www.army.mil, 27 July 2023.
5 Alex Chun, 'How Spam Became a Staple of Asian Cuisine', *Smithsonian Magazine*, www.smithsonianmag.com, 9 June 2023.
6 Ibid.
7 'In Korea, Lunar New Year Isn't Complete Without a Can of SPAM', Hormel Foods, www.hormelfoods.com, 22 January 2019.
8 Grace M. Cho, 'Eating Military Base Stew', *Contexts*, XIII/3 (Summer 2014), pp. 38–9.
9 Ibid., pp. 38, 40.
10 Michael J. Seth, 'An Unpromising Recovery: South Korea's Post-Korean War Economic Development: 1953–1961', *Central Asia,* XVII/3 (Winter 2013), pp. 42–5.
11 Ibid.
12 CJ Heritage, 'Part 7: The Evolution of Spam into a Popular Korean Dish', CJ Newsroom, https://newsroom.cj.net, 18 April 2023.
13 Jae-hee Choi, 'It's Seollal, and You've Got Spam', *Korean Herald*, www.koreaherald.com, 22 January 2023.

14 CJ CheilJedang, 'SPAM', www.cj.co.kr/en/brands/spam, accessed 3 August 2024.
15 CJ CheilJedang, 'SPAM Sawnmul Set', YouTube, www.youtube.com, accessed 31 July 2024.
16 Choi, 'It's Seollal'.
17 'Karrot', *Karrot*, https://karrotmarket.com, accessed 5 August 2024; 'Joonggonara', *Naver Café*, https://cafe.naver.com, accessed 5 August 2025.
18 Choi, 'It's Seollal'.

6 SPAM's Longevity and Enduring Appeal

1 See Cori Phelan, 'Hormel Foods Corp. v. Jim Henson Productions, Inc., 73 F.3d 497 (2d Cir. 1996)', *DePaul Journal of Art, Technology and Intellectual Property Law*, VI/2 (Spring 2016), pp. 313–16.
2 See Jaime Sunwoo's Specially Processed American Me website, https://speciallyprocessed.com/about.html, accessed 5 October 2024; see also Florence Fabricant, 'The Meaning of SPAM, Onstage', *New York Times*, www.nytimes.com, 31 January 2022.
3 See SPAM Haiku Archive, https://web.mit.edu, accessed 3 August 2024.
4 See the 'SPAM Sonnet (Sponnet) Page', 'SPAM Limericks (Spamerick) Archive', 'Other SPAM Poetry Forms', at the SPAM Haiku Archive, https://web.mit.edu, accessed 3 August 2024.
5 'Lake Speed's the Name, Driving Fast the Game', www.postbulletin.com, 18 June 1996.
6 See *Austin Daily Herald*, '75 Years of SPAM', 1 July 2012.
7 'SPAM Jamboree, Austin', www.postbulletin.com, 9 September 1992; 'Minnesota: SPAM Festival (Local Legacies: Celebrating Community Roots)', Library of Congress, https://webarchive.loc.gov, accessed 3 August 2024.
8 Jess Fleming, 'SPAM Recipe Contest Winners Include Monkey Bread, Nuggets', *Pioneer Press* (St Paul), www.twincities.com, 13 March 2018.

9 Matt Largey, 'What Ever Happened to Austin's "Spamarama"', ATXplained, Kut Kutx Studios, https://kutkutx.studio, 14 March 2019.
10 Britny Eubank, 'SPAMtastic News: SPAMarama Returns to Austin This Weekend', KVUE ABC, www.kvue.com, 2 April 2022.
11 Smithsonian Channel, 'How this Town Celebrates Your Favorite Canned Food', www.youtube.com, accessed 3 August 2024.
12 'Luncheon Style Meat', UnMeat, https://meetunmeat.us, accessed 3 August 2024.
13 'SPAM Sales Sizzle Sky-High During Pandemic', Hormel Foods, www.hormelfoods.com, 18 September 2020.
14 Marie Genries, 'Food, Water and Masks: South Korea's COVID-19 Quarantine Kits', https://observers.france24.com, 3 May 2022; 'SPAM: Food + War + Memory in a Can', *BBC Radio 4-The Food Programme*, www.bbc.co.uk, 1 May 2022.
15 Rob Wile, 'SPAM Donates 264,000 Cans of Meat Product Valued at $1 Million to Maui Wildfire Victims', *NBC News*, www.nbcnews.com, 17 August 2023.

7 SPAMtown USA

1 'Austin Plant – Plant Production Jobs – Hormel Foods', Hormel Foods, www.hormelfoods.com.
2 Ibid.
3 Mike Hughlett, 'More than 200 at Quality Pork, Hormel in Austin Test Positive for COVID-19', *Minneapolis Star Tribune*, www.startribune.com, 5 June 2020.
4 'SPAM Sales Sizzle Sky-High During Pandemic', Hormel Foods, www.hormelfoods.com, 18 September 2020.
5 'Hormel Foods Prepares, Donates Meals to Mower County Senior Center Members', *Austin Daily Herald*, www.austindailyherald.com, 19 March 2020.

Select Bibliography

American Dream, film, dir. Barbara Kopple et al., Channel 4/ Miramax (1992)

Atkins, P. J., 'Communal Feeding in War Time: British Restaurants, 1940–1947', in *Food and War in Twentieth Century Europe*, ed. Ina Zweiniger-Bargielowska, Rachel Duffett and Alain Drouard (London, 2011), pp. 139–54

BBC, 'SPAM: Food + War + Memory in a Can', *BBC Radio 4- The Food Programme*, 1 May 2022, www.bbc.co.uk

Bentley, Amy, *Eating for Victory: Food Rationing and the Politics of Domesticity*, (Champaign, IL, 1998)

Cho, Grace M., 'Eating Military Base Stew', *Contexts*, XIII/3 (Summer 2014), pp. 38–9

Cho, John, *Spam-Ku: Tranquil Reflections on Luncheon Loaf* (New York, 1998)

Dougherty, Richard, *In Quest of Quality: Hormel's First 75 Years* (St Paul, MN, 1966)

Hormel, George A., *The Open Road: Autobiography of George A. Hormel* (Austin, MN, 2019)

Hormel, *The Squeal: Hormel News-Magazine* (1937–45)

Kimball, Warren F., *The Most Unsordid Act: Lend-Lease, 1939–1941* (Baltimore, MD, 1969)

Koikari, Mire, 'Love! Spam: Food, Military and Empire in Post-The Second World War Okinawa', in *Devouring Japan: Global Perspectives on Japanese Culinary Identity*, ed. Nancy K. Stalker (Oxford, 2018), pp. 171–86

Lend-Lease Bill (10 January 1941), records of the U.S. House of Representatives, HR 77A-D13, Record Group 233, National Archives

Lund, Doniver Adolph, *The Hormel Legacy: 100 Years of Quality* (Austin, MN, 1991)

Ordonio, Cassie, 'It's No Secret Hawai-i Loves SPAM. But Health Experts Fear Its Long-Term Risks', Hawai'i Public Radio, www.hawaiipublicradio.org, 22 May 2023

Patten, Marguerite, *SPAM: The Cookbook* (London, 2001)

Rogers, Robert F., *Destiny's Landfall: A History of Guam* (Honolulu, HI, 1995)

Roodhouse, Mark, *Black Market Britain, 1939–1955* (Oxford, 2013)

Spam-Ku, independent film, written and dir. Steven K. Tsuchida (2004), https://vimeo.com

'Spam', *Monty Python's Flying Circus*, *BBC*, written by Terry Jones and Michael Palin (1970)

Spamalot, dir. Mike Nichols, music John Du Prez and Eric Idle, lyrics Eric Idle (2005)

Sinclair, Upton, *The Jungle* (New York, 1906)

Spring, Kelly A., '"Today We Have All Got to be Fighting Fit": The Interconnectivity of Gender Roles in British Food Rationing Propaganda during the Second World War', *Gender and History*, XXXII/2 (July 2020), pp. 320–40

Taylor, Horace, *How Shall Lend-Lease Accounts Be Settled?* (Washington, DC, 1945)

Taylor, Victoria, 'SPAM is a "Heart-Warming" Gift in South Korea', *New York Daily News*, www.nydailynews.com, 10 January 2019

Wile, Rob, 'SPAM Donates 264,000 Cans of Meat Product Valued at $1 million to Maui Wildfire Victims', NBC News, www.nbcnews.com, 17 August 2023

Wyman, Carolyn, *SPAM: A Biography* (New York, 1999)

Zweiniger-Bargielowska, Ina, *Austerity in Britain: Rationing, Controls, and Consumption, 1939–1955* (Oxford, 2000)

Websites and Associations

Global Hormel and Hormel-Affiliated Websites

SPAM, www.spam.com
SPAM UK, www.spam-uk.com
Okinawa Hormel (in Japanese), https://okinawahormel.co.jp
CJ CheilJedang (in Korean), www.cj.co.kr

Social Media Sites

Facebook: 'SPAM'
X: '@SPAMbrand'
TikTok: 'SPAM® Brand'
Instagram: 'The SPAM® Brand'
Pinterest: 'SPAM® Brand'
YouTube: 'SPAM Brand'

Festivals Dedicated to and/or Selling SPAM

SPAM Jam, www.spamjamhawaii.com
Minnesota State Fair, www.mnstatefair.org

SPAM in Literature

SPAM Haiku Archive, https://web.mit.edu

Acknowledgements

Although this is a monograph, it was by no means created alone or in isolation. Many friends and family aided, supported and, most of all, fed me along the way, making this volume in the Edible series possible. First and foremost, many, many thanks go to Marci Freedman, who initially sent me the information about the series and who urged me to turn my research on SPAM into a book.

There is a wealth of material on SPAM in the archives, in print and digital format. The many and varied resources of the Library of Congress provided the foundation for my research on the processed pork product. My thanks go to the staff at the Library of Congress for facilitating my many book orders and offering me a wonderful environment in which to delve into this particular food history. My heartfelt thanks go to the staff at the Mower County Historical Society in Austin, Minnesota. Specifically, Executive Director Randal J. Forster, who kindly took the time to tell me the history of the organization and to show me around the original Hormel building on the Society's grounds. A special thank you and much appreciation goes to the Society's Research and Archives Manager, Sue Doocy. Sue went above and beyond to organize my visit and granted me invaluable access to their abundant and diverse collection of Hormel and Hormel-related materials.

Along this journey, many people have expressed their interest and enthusiasm for this project, which spurred me on and enabled me to bring it to fruition. Because of the ubiquity of SPAM, everyone I talked to had a story about the tinned good, whether positive or negative. Hearing these stories gave me a greater appreciation for the food and provided me with a deeper understanding of its importance in a global context. Many thanks go to Betsy Wendt, who was enthusiastic about the research from the moment she heard about it and who provided me with the limited-edition SPAM Figgy Pudding to help propel my research forward. A large thank you also goes to my Korean teacher, Kyechong Fitts, with whom I had great discussions about the role of SPAM in South Korea, past and present, and who shared with me stories of the Korean War from her own family's history. She also kindly read an earlier draft of Chapter Five on the history of SPAM in South Korea. Thank you also goes to my ESL student Miki Otani, who provided me with invaluable information about SPAM in Japan and the various ways that it is incorporated into Japanese dishes, particularly those eaten by Okinawans.

Finally, I would like to express my immense gratitude and appreciation to the lovely ladies of the SPAM Reading Group: my mom, Judy Spring; Judith Plotz and Caroline Barron. I have bombarded and overloaded these three women with my constant discoveries, deliberations and consternations about SPAM during the span of the project. At this point, they know almost as much as I do about the pork product. This and many other reasons made them the perfect people to read and comment on my manuscript. A heartfelt thank-you to the three of you and much, much love.

Photo Acknowledgements

The author and publishers wish to express their thanks to the sources listed below for illustrative material and/or permission to reproduce it. Some locations of works are also given below, in the interest of brevity:

Buffalo and Erie County Public Library: p. 14; Cornell University Library, Ithaca, NY: p. 22; Flickr: pp. 11 (photo freezelight, CC BY-SA 2.0), 67 (photo bonbon671, CC BY 2.0), 70 (photo Lorie Shaull, CC BY 2.0), 80 (photo Lifetime Travelmates, CC BY-SA 2.0), 81 (*above*; photo Maggie Hoffman, CC BY 2.0), 82 (photo Korea.net/Korean Culture and Information Service (Jeon Han), CC BY-SA 2.0), 87 (photo anokarina, CC BY-SA 2.0), 88 (photo T. Tseng, CC BY 2.0), 90 (photo Eduardo Unda-Sanzana, CC BY 2.0), 96 (photo Lorie Shaull, CC BY 2.0), 98 (photo Wisconsin Denizen, CC BY 2.0), 108 (photo Lorie Shaull, CC BY 2.0); Florida Atlantic University Libraries, Boca Raton: p. 28; Franklin D. Roosevelt Library, Hyde Park, NY: p. 20; Imperial War Museum, London: pp. 38, 41, 49; Library of Congress, Prints and Photographs Division, Washington, DC: pp. 27, 29 (photo John Vachon), 35 (photo Ann Rosener), 56; Manitowoc County Historical Society, WI: p. 31; Minnesota Historical Society, Saint Paul: pp. 17, 34; National Archives at College Park, MD: pp. 58, 59, 62, 64 (photo Signal Corps Archive), 74, 75; National Gallery of Art, Washington, DC: p. 51; Pixabay: pp. 6 (photo Tracey Pocock), 84 (photo Sharon Ang); private collection: p. 61; Shutterstock.com: pp. 69 (junpinzon), 107 (Steve Cukrov); photos Kelly A. Spring: pp. 53, 66, 68, 102, 110; Wikimedia Commons: pp. 32 (photo $ILENCE

DOO6OOD, CC BY-SA 3.0), 71 (photo Dllu, CC BY-SA 4.0), 81 (*below*; photo Phonet, public domain), 85 (photo Melsj, CC BY-SA 4.0), 101 (photo Msuaic HWAIE Dungia, CC BY-SA 4.0), 106 and 109 (photos Darbo2, CC BY-SA 4.0), 111 (photo Myotus, CC BY-SA 4.0).

Index

italic numbers refer to illustrations; **bold** to recipes